BAD
SANTAS

BAD SANTAS

AND OTHER CREEPY CHRISTMAS CHARACTERS

PAUL HAWKINS

**SIMON &
SCHUSTER**

London · New York · Sydney · Toronto · New Delhi

A CBS COMPANY

First published in Great Britain by Simon & Schuster UK Ltd, 2013
A CBS COMPANY

Copyright © 2013 by Paul Hawkins

The right of Paul Hawkins to be identified as the author of this work
has been asserted in accordance with sections 77 and 78 of
the Copyright, Designs and Patents Act, 1988.

Jacket and interior illustrations copyright © Melissa Four

1 3 5 7 9 10 8 6 4 2

Simon & Schuster UK Ltd
1st Floor
222 Gray's Inn Road
London WC1X 8HB

www.simonandschuster.co.uk

Simon & Schuster Australia,
Sydney

Simon & Schuster India,
New Delhi

A CIP catalogue record for this book
is available from the British Library.

The publishers have made every effort to contact those holding rights
reproduced in this book. Where this has not been possible the publishers
will be glad to hear from those who recognise their material.

ISBN HB: 978-1-47112-986-5
ISBN Ebook: 978-1-47112-985-8

Typeset by M Rules
Printed and bound by CPI Group (UK) Ltd, Croydon, CR0 4YY

For my nephew, Charlie. May he always be safe from the clutches of the Christmas Cat.

Contents

The Night Before Christmas

It's just after midnight on Christmas Eve in a remote village somewhere in England. Even though everyone has sung songs and sent postcards dreaming of a White Christmas, those never seem to happen in England. Instead, it is raining.

It is really, really raining.

Hailstones smash against the ground, the thunder roars like a demon and lightning flashes out from the night sky. In a tiny bedroom in a converted loft, a little girl lies in bed clutching a silver teddy bear. She is trying to sleep but, between the excitement over Christmas and the terror of the storm, she instead huddles in bed listening. Wondering if *he* is going to arrive.

Without warning, she hears a tremendous crash. Something has landed on the roof. All above her is the clatter of animal hooves, the screeching and scratching of a heavy object being dragged across the tiles and the sound of an old man's laughter rolling across the night air. A laughter that never seems to end.

Within the space of a peel of thunder and a sharp flicker of lightning, the sleigh and the hooves grind to a halt. Now, aside from the rain and irritated grunts from the animals, the only sounds are the footsteps and that never-ending laughter.

The little girl lies in the dark listening to the footsteps and tracking their path across the roof. They rattle across to the other side and she is struck by the realisation – *he* is going to come down the chimney.

She lies in bed, tightly clutching her teddy bear, listening to the sounds of grunting and growling as he squeezes his way down the chimney and into the house. He gives a howl of pain and she begins to really wish she had a lock on her door. The artificial tree in the lounge is too small to fit presents underneath, and so she thinks nervously about the empty sack at the end of her bed, which must be his final destination.

Snapped back from her thoughts, she realises he has emerged from the chimney and she can hear him moving around downstairs. Downstairs in her home. He stops to guzzle whisky and mince pies. She hears him greedily wolf them down and, not long after that, footsteps thump through the lounge and to the bottom of the stairs.

And up the first step.

And up the second step. Laughing all the way.

Outside the rain hammers down and the thunder growls like a wounded beast.

The third step, the fourth and the fifth.

Above her, an animal grunts and squeals. Below her, those clumping feet continue to climb.

Up to the top of the stairs, then slowly across the landing until they stop outside her door.

She peers out from under the covers as the handle on the door begins to turn. The door squeaks open. Seconds later, he is in her room.

He moves towards the end of her bed. It is far too dark to see anything but still she knows this because she can hear him.

Suddenly, there is another flash of lightning and it illuminates a wild, bearded man with an enormous bush of beard and a blood-red suit.

He has arrived.

Preface – Here Comes Santa Claus . . .

Imagine, if you will, that a committee has called upon a focus group to design a new international children's folk hero: a popular hero for a major celebration who can appeal to children and adults alike; a figure who can resonate all around the world from Texas to Thailand, from Austria to Australia, from South America to Scandinavia; a figure who, despite his status as a symbol of a Christmas celebration, can appeal to Christians and non-Christians alike; a figure so ubiquitous and flexible he can be used to spearhead religious celebrations or to sell children's toys, cigarettes or even sex.

If a committee were to design such a character, then it is highly unlikely they would propose a solitary old man who spends most of the year in isolated retreat at the North Pole accompanied only by elves and reindeer, save for one night a year when he breaks into houses and leaves gifts for children.

Admittedly, this is partly due to a modern change in social attitudes towards solitary old men. Whereas once age and wisdom were valued, we now see the energy of youth as a more appealing quality. What's more, the media has repeatedly revealed to us that the eccentric old men in whom we used to put our trust – from politicians to religious figures to celebrities – may have sinister motives. What once seemed enigmatic and mysterious now seems creepy and odd. But, even beyond the modern temptation to find evil intentions in what was once deemed innocent, there's something weird and wonderful about a reindeer-riding, globetrotting housebreaking interloper with a mystical workshop and an army of elves. To me, it has always suggested a story that's far more bizarre and interesting than the benign, slightly dull, kindly old man that the names Father Christmas or Santa Claus often summon to mind.

Before I started researching this book, my understanding of the history of Father Christmas or Santa Claus went roughly as follows: a Turkish bishop called St Nicholas used to give Christmas presents to children, leaving the gifts in children's shoes and stockings. This tradition was preserved and commemorated over time, especially in the Netherlands and Germany. Somehow or other this tradition spread across the world, and eventually St Nicholas became Father Christmas, possibly getting his suit designed by Coca-Cola in the process.

This leaves a lot more questions than answers. Who was St Nicholas and why on earth did he start to leave presents in shoes? How exactly does a bishop leaving presents in shoes lead to a fat and jolly man in red scampering up and down chimneys? And why are there nearly a thousand years between St Nicholas's death and his first appearances as a Christmas figure giving out gifts?

An alternative explanation is that Santa Claus never had anything to do with Christianity at all and, like many other Christmas traditions, he was simply a continuation of pagan rituals – sixth-century pagans in many countries would dress in furs and a beard and travel from home to home, presenting themselves as Old Man Winter. They would receive food and hospitality in the belief this would give homeowners luck. The argument goes that, over the Middle Ages, Old Man Winter became Father Christmas, and the link with St Nicholas was simply added to give the sheen of Christian respectability so it conformed and merged comfortably with official religious beliefs.

Again this does not feel quite right. Certainly it's true that Old Man Winter has been (and remains) a popular figure throughout many parts of Europe, and many aspects of the English character of Father Christmas may well have developed from this custom. But the traditional English Father Christmas that existed up until Victorian times and the modern-day Santa Claus are very different characters.

What's more, ancient customs that we now talk about as 'pagan' are often little understood. Few people in those societies could read or write, and much of what we understand of pagan rituals comes from people writing about them from the Middle Ages onwards – and often much later than that – by which time they may have changed immeasurably from ancient times. And many of the first people to write about pagan traditions were actually Christians (who were usually criticising them for not being holy enough), so may not have been the most reliable sources.

These Christian writers also had a tendency to dismiss anything that didn't fit their beliefs as wild pagan behaviour, regardless of its religious origin (or whether it had a religious origin at all). So whilst, say, the masked drunken revelry at a Christmas celebration of the Middle Ages clearly had little to do with Christ, some of the customs involved might have simply been hedonism for hedonism's sake rather than related to religious beliefs. Nonetheless, midwinter festivals existed long before the birth of Christianity, and many of the traditions and features of those festivals are kept alive in the modern Christmas.

The extent and way in which Christmas is celebrated has changed over time. No Christian winter festival existed until the fourth century, at which point Christmas gradually began to take over from existing festivals like Saturnalia and January Kalends in the Roman Empire and eventually from Yule in Scandinavia. The new feast – liberally mixed with non-Christian customs – grew in popularity over the next thousand years. A strict backlash against public rowdiness, drunkenness and 'unchristian' behaviour led to the festival being reduced to a minor event – and even banned outright – during the seventeenth and eighteenth centuries, but Christmas was dramatically revived in Victorian times to the point where it became the massive global event that it remains today.

The Victorian Christmas included some ancient traditions but also invented a lot of new customs that have no clear link to either pagan or Christian Christmases past but nevertheless heavily shape how we celebrate Christmas now – Christmas cards, presents and (in England, at least) Christmas trees all date from this time. Even the idea of the 'Christmas spirit' and Christmas as a time for children are relatively recent innovations – there was little generosity and barely a role for children in the drunken medieval Christmas, where anarchy ruled and strangers were routinely tricked, assaulted and tormented in the name of amusement. Indeed, it was only when Christmas became sanitised in the Victorian age that kindness to children and goodwill to all men were placed at the centre of what Christmas was 'supposed' to be about. Nowadays we think of Charles Dickens and his Christmas books such as *A Christmas Carol* as being stories that attempt to preserve the tradition and meaning of Christmas but, in actual fact, Dickens was inventing traditions as much as he was preserving them.

This, of course, leads to a third possible explanation of Santa Claus – maybe the figure is simply an invention of the nineteenth century, and all the supposed links and parallels to the past are mere coincidences? Perhaps the modern Santa Claus is an American invention that subsequently proved so popular that his reputation and myths took hold across the world. It is true that a great deal of our traditions around Santa Claus – his work-shop, his elves and his home at the North Pole, to name a few – do date from the nineteenth century in America. What's more, 200 years elapsed between the first Dutch settlers in America and Washington Irving first writing about Santa Claus, and there is no evidence to suggest that the first Dutch settlers observed the traditional visits of St Nicholas that are said to have led to his creation.

Nonetheless, forefathers of Santa Claus clearly existed a long time before that. In the time of the Vikings, the Norse god Odin was said to ride a great eight-legged horse through the sky each Yule, throwing sweets to children. From the thirteenth century onwards tradition has it that St Nicholas visited houses in Europe on 6 December to pass judgement on children's behav-iour. Father Christmas defended English Christmas traditions in the face of Puritan protests in the sixteenth century, and all across medieval Europe a whole range of creepy characters stalked the midwinter landscape to seek out children to punish for being bad – and very occasionally reward them for being good. Even the imagery of reindeer, sled and chimneys may have its roots in the religious rituals of Sami shamans in the Arctic Circle.

It is hard to trace a direct line that links the traditions of Eur-ope with the traditions that sprang up in the US in the nineteenth century, but it is even harder to argue that there is no link at all. The Protestant Dutch settlers of New Amsterdam may not have brought St Nicholas with them, but the name Santa Claus clearly comes from Sinterklaas, the Dutch name for St Nicholas, and the character that emerged had strong parallels with St Nicholas and a host of other characters – even if Santa represented them in a highly sanitised form.

By the middle of the twentieth century the influence of American culture was so great that their version of Santa Claus had spread across Europe, sometimes replacing existing mythology and sometimes combining with it to create a local version of Santa Claus, but nonetheless one heavily in thrall to the jolly man in red who lived with his elves at the North Pole. Much as the North American grey squirrel has become so dominant in the UK and parts of Europe that the native red squirrel has retreated to the periphery, so too have native European Christmas traditions of gift-givers been forced into retreat by the ubiquity of Santa Claus.

The purpose of this book, however, is not to criticise Santa's influence – or indeed to attempt to hark back to a mythical 'better time' when Christmas was closer to its roots – but rather to highlight the range of fantastic myths and folk stories that have existed around Christmas within Europe and across the world. Even in my early thirties, I still get ridiculously excited by Christmas and look forward to one day telling my own children about Santa Claus, but myths such as the Yule Lads, the Krampus and the Christmas Cat are utterly brilliant, twisted and compelling creations, and I'd hope that Christmas has a place for those stories in addition to the story of a jolly man coming down the chimney and dropping off presents.

Throughout the book I will refer to the modern-day Father Christmas as Santa Claus. This may frustrate some readers, but the reason for this is that Father Christmas is a unique character with a history and tradition long before his association with the version of Christmas gift-giver that emerged as Santa Claus or Father Christmas in Victorian times. Thus, in order to save the two characters from being confused, and to reflect the US origins of the latter character, I have decided to stick to the American name. I don't like it any more than you do.

For the ease of the contemporary reader, I have also taken the decision to refer to the geographical areas of both Germany and Italy by their modern names, even when referring to a period before they were united. Both these countries were actually divided into a number of states and city states up until the nineteenth century, but I think that using the modern names throughout will make the narrative easier to follow.

Some of my research has come from published books, some from blogs and the Internet, and some directly from people who've grown up in a particular country and were keen to share their traditions. I am grateful especially to my friends Juha Niesniemi and Will Vaughan, as well as Will's friend Gudjon Olaffson for providing help with translations of Finnish and Icelandic texts into English and thus giving me access to material that, in many cases, has not previously been published in the English language.

Folk stories differ from region to region and from teller to teller, so some readers may have heard these stories before in slightly different forms. Like any traditional storyteller, I have occasionally added my own embellishments to make the stories relevant to the modern reader. Nonetheless, my intention is to capture the style and spirit in which these stories would originally have been told.

Introduction

In the Bleak Midwinter

Although the mention of Christmas traditionally conjures up images of carol singers, parties and families gathering round the tree together to exchange gifts, it has not always been a wholly joyful occasion. For centuries, people across Europe believed the twelve days of Christmas to be the time when devils, demons, ghosts and witches were free to wander the Earth searching for doomed souls to feast upon.

In Greece, the twelve days of Christmas was the time that malevolent goblins called Kallikantzaroi could venture above ground to spread strife and mischief amongst the population. They stole things, destroyed property and even abducted children born over the Christmas period in order to turn them into one of their own. In Finland, an evil goat called Joulupukki would turn up at houses just before Yuletide to demand gifts and punish evil children. In parts of Italy and Germany, the witch Perchta would – just like Santa – enter houses through the chimney over the Christmas season. Unlike Santa, however, she did not leave presents for children but instead ripped their intestines out and replaced them with straw and stones. Icelandic households were tormented by thirteen evil trolls and a child-eating cat, whilst any Serb who found himself out alone late at night in winter might be turned into a slave of the malevolent Karakoncolos, who would leap on his back and ride him around the isolated rural roads as if he were a horse.

And so it was that, from country to country, the midwinter visitors of the past were not kindly old gentlemen aiming to reward children with presents but demonic creatures who wanted to gleefully and sadistically torment and punish children and adults alike.

At first glance, it seems odd that Christmas – supposedly a joyful celebration of the birth of Jesus Christ – should produce so many terrible, twisted characters. However, the celebration of Christmas has traditionally been about more than simply the birth of the baby Jesus. There are no references to the actual date or season of Jesus's birth in the New Testament, but it is surely not mere coincidence that the date on which Christmas began to be celebrated in the fourth century corresponds with the time of traditional pagan celebrations such as Saturnalia, Yule and Modraniht (or Mothers' Night) – a night when pagans would make a blood sacrifice to honour the memory of their female ancestors.

It is easy to find a plausible motive for Christians appropriating these dates and piggybacking on existing festivities. From an early point, Christian missionaries realised it was far easier to convert people by finding common ground between existing traditions and new Christian practices – a common tactic was to take existing traditions and customs of the people they wanted to convert and simply re-interpret them with a more Biblical explanation. Co-opting Yule as a celebration of the birth of Christ was a far easier way of getting new converts on board than trying to popularise a new celebration. What's more, the symbolism of the birth of renewed hope at the bleakest time of the year – with its clear links to the message of the birth of hope in bleak times that's central to the nativity story – probably made it too tempting to resist.

Make no mistake, midwinter truly was a bleak time. In the Northern Hemisphere the twelve of days of Christmas coincide more or less with the shortest days, the darkest nights and the harshest weather of the year – a time the Turkish used to term 'the dreadful cold'. The only sources of light were basic oil lamps, candles and fires – all of which were unreliable and left much of the room awash with shadows, in which any danger, real or imagined, could be lurking. As people huddled together in their homes on long winter's nights, surrounded by the sounds of the terrible weather outside and the eeriness of a room full of shadows, it is hardly surprising that they began to tell each other stories of the wicked, terrible things that those shadows might contain.

And certainly great terrors did lurk in the darkness of winter. Food was scarce and, even with a fire roaring in one corner, homes were freezing cold – often fatally so. The elderly and the young were especially at risk and it would not be at all unusual or unexpected for people to wake up in the morning and discover that a neighbour, a relative or perhaps even a child had perished during the night. The deaths would be cruel, sudden and seemingly random and meaningless. In this light, stories of monsters stealing into houses unseen and taking loved ones away seems an understandable way to put a name to a nameless threat and allow people to discuss their fears. If Christmas and other midwinter celebrations provided relief from the long, bleak and barren winter months, then the demons and devils of these folk tales were expressions of the physical and metaphorical darkness that the winter months created. Christmas was a time of endurance as well as celebration, and surviving the dangerous beasts that roamed the Christmas period was a symbolic triumph over the 'dreadful cold' and the start of journey toward the spring.

The stories people used to tell each other form the basis of this book. These are tales that will have been told from person to person and from generation to generation – perhaps seated around a fire on a cold winter's night or to while away the time whilst carrying out tough winter's work – and they tell us a lot about the beliefs and fears of ordinary people in Europe and across the world through the ages. Most of these legends and myths stemmed from folk culture, which is to say that they were stories ordinary people would pass on and tell one another rather than accounts that stemmed from people in positions of political power or religious authority – indeed, figures like the Krampus, the Yule Lads and even St Nicholas himself have received political and religious censure at one time or another due to their perceived subversiveness. There have been attempts by religions and government to control these stories and introduce myths of their own, but these have tended to backfire spectacularly.

As few people could read or write, tales were told and retold countless times before they were ever written down. They were related from memory and each storyteller would forget or disregard certain details and perhaps add flourishes of their own. Even within the same countries and the same communities, they could be told in a multitude of different ways. An accomplished and respected storyteller would have their own signature way of telling a story, whilst each family or each group of friends would have their own unique take on each tale.

This is important because storytelling is, first and foremost, a social activity. Sharing information and anecdotes is a huge part of building friendships and relationships. We share secrets and stories about ourselves in order to let friends and loved ones feel close to us, and we conceal that information from people we dislike to keep them at a distance. We tell stories about other people too, affectionately letting our friends know what other people we like have been up to and – much as most of us prefer not to admit – gossiping about people we don't like. Our shared stories and histories are a huge part of what makes our identities and relationships. Witness how a group of close friends can collapse into hysterics at the merest reminder of a past hilarity. The stories people told each other during the winter, and the way that they were told, would have played a huge part in deciding who was inside and who was outside a particular community.

The stories played another important role too. In the dangerous conditions of winter, with the threats of the cold and the lack of food and the increased risk that the darkness could bring, the stories provided warnings and guidance about acceptable and 'safe' ways to behave. In the same way a modern TV campaign warns you of the dangers of drink-driving by creating a world where anyone who drinks and drives is met with the worst consequences possible – imprisonment, permanent disablement or death – many of the stories in this book use the threat of supernatural punishment to persuade people to avoid dangerous behaviour: keep your house warm; keep your children safe; don't go out alone at night.

The medieval St Nicholas – not unlike the modern Santa Claus – rewarded children for being 'good' and obeying their parents. Nowadays this focus on good behaviour has become a way to affectionately tease children, but in the past this obedience was a protection against much greater threats. With St Nicholas these threats were spiritual ones. Infant mortality was high and the Church preached a literal version of eternal damnation in Hell. Parents anxiously urged their children to learn scripture and behave piously – if the worst should happen to them, no parents wanted their child to suffer eternal torment.

Other myths provided protection from more tangible physical dangers. The idea of demons wandering the roads at winter prevented a child wandering off into the cold and darkness, threats of wood-dwelling goblins or monsters kept children away from thick woodlands where they might get lost, and threats of evil water-dwelling spirits kept children away from ponds and rivers where they might drown.

It is hard to be sure of the extent to which adults literally believed these myths to be true and these creatures to be real. These were superstitious times when devils, monsters and supernatural creatures were taken far more seriously than today but, much like modern horror stories, tales also existed for entertainment on dark winter nights. Just as you can enjoy *Alien*, *The Omen* or *Dawn of the Dead* without literally believing in slavering space monsters, devil children or zombies, so too people could enjoy the stories of mysterious, terrifying Christmas creatures even if they did not literally believe these creatures existed.

Perhaps the best comparison is the way that at Hallowe'en – which has now taken over from Christmas as the chosen night for the dead, the cryptozoological and the evil to wander the Earth – we might sit around telling each other ghost stories. Some people will believe every word, others will remain firmly sceptical, and others still will simply enjoy the thrill of being frightened.

But many of them will go to bed still secretly wondering about what strange, ferocious beasts might be hiding in the darkness, ready to pounce on them in the middle of the night. It seems likely that most of the creatures in this book are long gone, if they even ever existed at all.

But who knows exactly what there is lurking in the shadows?

1

Four Miracles and a Grave-Robbing

St Nicholas (Turkey)

It is widely believed that the story of Christmas starts with St Nicholas. To many Christians, he is unquestionably the genesis of Father Christmas: a kindly old priest who marked the birth of Christ by giving money and gifts to needy children of his parish and, in doing so, kicked off a tradition of gift-giving and Christmas charity that has survived for nearly two thousand years. From Little Saint Nick to Jolly Old St Nicholas he's been the subject of stories and popular songs. The poem popularly known as 'The Night Before Christmas' – which popularised Santa Claus – is more accurately titled 'A Visit from St Nicholas'. Even Santa's name derives from the Dutch for St Nicholas. Clearly St Nick is a major player in the Santa stakes.

Some would go even further. St Nicholas isn't just the original Santa but perhaps the better Santa too. As a Christian saint he's more connected to the religious aspects of Christmas. As a historical figure that predates Christmas commercialism, he more closely embodies 'traditional' Christmas values such as giving to the poor without expectation of reward. While the modern-day Santa Claus is continually corrupted by commercial use and the greed of big corporations, St Nicholas remains untainted by advertisements and represents a simpler and more virtuous age.

All of this is very nice but, unless you get a vicarious thrill out of hearing about kindness, virtue and decency, it's not terribly exciting. Certainly it's not easy to see how such a figure fits into a book called *Bad Santas*. Where's the drama? Where's the terror? Where's the blood and gore?

Luckily, if you dig a little deeper into the legend of St Nicholas, you quickly uncover tales of cannibalism, prostitution, grave-robbing and kidnapping. The legends tend to cast him as a saviour from – rather than a perpetrator of – evil, gruesome and macabre acts, but nonetheless the stories associated with his life are a far cry from the mundane, benign pleasantness that is so often associated with him.

I use the words 'legends' and 'stories' because the actual established facts about the life of St Nicholas are few and far between. None of his own writings or sermons remain and the earliest account of his life on record was written 350 years after his death. What's more, its writer, Michael the Archimandrite, is otherwise unknown and, like any good journalist, doesn't reveal his sources. What we are left with is an enormous number of myths and legends about Nicholas, many of which were developed or embellished as the saint's popularity grew during the Middle Ages.

So what do we know? It seems certain that St Nicholas was known during his lifetime as Niklaos of Myra and that he was a fourth-century bishop in a town in what is now southwest Turkey (but was then a part of Greece).[1] In the years after Niklaos's death, Myra built its first Church of St Nicholas, which suggests that the saint already had a local reputation by the time Michael wrote about him.

Stories suggest that he was born to wealthy parents and died on 6 December in an unknown year. This date is still celebrated as St Nicholas's Day in many countries. Beyond these sketchy 'facts', the veracity of almost every other aspect of his life is up for debate. Some scholars question whether there is sufficient evidence that he even existed at all.[2]

Things are made even more confusing by the fact that many

21

parts of Michael's life of Nicholas bear remarkable similarities to myths about other saints and religious figures. This is not unusual – copyright laws did not exist and writers of hagiographies would often purloin every miracle they could find and attribute it to 'their' saint in an effort to prove the sanctity of their subject. However, it does underline that we are dealing with myths, stories and legends rather than proven reality. Fortunately, this entire book is about myths, stories and legends so, as long as you have your pinch of salt at the ready, I will continue.

Stories tell us Niklaos was an extremely well-behaved child who, from an early age, showed a surprising degree of holiness. Shortly after his birth, he stood up in the bath and appeared to bow his head in prayer. In a particularly curious move, he showed his love of Christ by refusing to suckle at his mother's breast on a Friday – a level of detail that really makes me wish Michael *had* revealed his sources. Nonetheless, Niklaos grew up enjoying the trappings of wealth until his parents died whilst he was still young. This meant he inherited their vast wealth, but the shock of the deaths deepened his commitment to Christianity and led to him giving away all his worldly possessions in an act of faith. Some accounts suggest that Niklaos was one of the many Christians imprisoned by the Roman Emperor Diocletian from AD 302 to AD 304.[3] If so, that would have made him approximately thirty years old on his release.

It is said that Niklaos became a bishop by chance – or divine intervention, if you will – despite having no formal training or previous employment within the Church. The Bishop of Myra had died and the Council of Bishops met in his church in order to choose his successor. As they sat debating the virtues of the various candidates, proceedings were suddenly interrupted by a mysterious voice that commanded them to appoint the next person called

Nicholas to walk through the church door. The Council took this to be the voice of God. A few minutes later Niklaos wandered into the church as a layman and he walked out again as a bishop.

St Nicholas versus the Cannibals

There are an extraordinary number of myths about St Nicholas and two of them are particularly interesting. Both stories involve his role as a protector of children and young people – a common theme of stories associated with St Nick. The first of these is fabulously macabre ...

There was a famine in the town of Myra and it had grown so severe the town was almost out of food. In particular, there was a severe shortage of meat. The people were going hungry. Mothers had no food to serve up to their children, butchers had no food to sell to their customers and the inns were going out of business as they could not feed and provide for their guests.

One of the hungry citizens of Myra was a mother with three young sons. She had given all the food she had to her children and she and her husband had gone hungry. But now the food had run out and there was not a crumb to be found. The husband brought in a decent wage, but all the money in the world would not have changed the fact that there was no food left to buy in any of the markets. Things were desperate and the mother knew the children had to eat soon but she was exhausted from the meals she had skipped and had become too tired to leave the house. So one day, when her husband was away at work, she gave her three sons some money and sent them out to look for food.

The boys went out and promised they would be home by the late afternoon but – when their father returned from his day at work – the children still had not come back.

The mother was worried but the father tried to reassure her. With no food in Myra, the boys must have had to travel to the next town in order to find something to eat. Surely, he said, they would be back by nightfall.

Night fell and the boys still had not returned. The father too was now beginning to worry but still he thought it best to reassure his wife. Perhaps the next town had no food either; the boys might have had to travel to the next town but one in order to find something to eat. Surely, he said, they would be back by midnight.

Midnight came and there was still no sign of the boys. On the inside, the father was extremely concerned, but he knew there was nothing he could do until the morning except to give his wife reassurance. Perhaps the famine had grown so great that even the next town but one had no food; the boys could have had to travel to the next town along again. Surely, absolutely surely, he said, they would be back by sunrise.

But the sun rose and the boys were nowhere to be seen. Unable to hide his concerns any longer, the terrified father asked his wife what she thought they should do. She said that the only option was to go and see the local bishop – and, of course, the hero of our story – to seek his help.

Being the helpful, kind and indeed saintly man that he was, Nicholas reassured the parents and agreed at once to look for the children. He enquired around the town. The people respected Nicholas and feared God, and perhaps they even cared about the safety of the children, and they were quick to tell him all they knew. His enquiries ultimately led

him to a local inn which, so he was told, three boys had been
seen to visit the previous afternoon. The bishop went to the
inn and, upon entering, encountered a frightened-looking
servant. At first the servant refused to speak, but Nicholas
calmly commanded him in the name of the Lord. Overcome
with fear and wonder, the servant told Nicholas that the
innkeeper had become so desperate for meat to serve his customers that he had lured the boys inside with the promise of
a good meal. However, he had instead locked them in the
cellar with the intention of killing them, chopping them up
and pickling them to sell as meat to his customers.

Nicholas was rather alarmed by this turn of events and he
hurried down to the cellar at once. When he got there, he
found the innkeeper clad in a blood-spattered apron and
clutching an enormous meat cleaver. Nicholas was shocked
by the horror that had unfolded, and perhaps even fearful
that he could be next, but nonetheless he calmly confronted
the innkeeper, telling him everything he knew and demanding a confession and repentance.

The innkeeper was flabbergasted by the bishop's knowledge of his actions. It did not occur to him to suspect that his
servant had been snitching on him, but instead he immediately assumed that God must have been watching him and
had sent Nicholas as an agent of retribution. The innkeeper
fell at the bishop's feet and repented for his terrible crimes.
However, he weepingly told Nicholas that he had arrived
too late. He had already killed the boys and, in order to preserve them, had sealed them in a barrel of saltwater.

The innkeeper showed Nicholas the barrel in question
and lifted the lid to allow the bishop to look upon the bodies
of the children – or perhaps more accurately at the pickled

meat that used to be the children – lying inside the barrel. The bishop managed to suppress his emotions as he laid his hands on each hunk of pickling meat and silently prayed. One by one the hunks of meat transformed into the three brothers, and one by one the three brothers spluttered back to life. After a few minutes out of the water, the boys looked for all the world as though no misfortune had ever befallen them. Nicholas returned the children to their parents and they went on to live happy, healthy lives.

Meanwhile, the innkeeper begged for forgiveness and Nicholas agreed to pardon him. He was so moved by his experience that, from that day forwards, he became a devout Christian and, no matter how bad the famine got, no child was ever pickled in his inn again.

This story originated in the Middle Ages and might be a misinterpretation of a medieval painting of St Nicholas intervening at a court to save three wrongly accused men from execution.[4]

Confusing three men in a courtroom with three children pickling in a barrel is a strange mistake to make. However, the painting was a top-down view of Nicholas standing at the foot of a round wooden tower, which the three men stood upon as they awaited their fate. The painter had represented St Nicholas's superiority to mere mortals by painting him as larger than the condemned men, so it looked like a fully grown adult stood next to a barrel of children. People saw the painting and, not knowing the tale, filled the blanks in for themselves as to what they thought the story represented. As a result, a whole new myth was born. True or not, this is not a bad analogy for how stories of both St Nicholas, and later Santa Claus, would spread around the world.

The Origins of Santa Claus

Although the tale of the three brothers links St Nicholas with helping and protecting children, it does not yet connect him to Christmas or a jolly man in red. However, another popular story about St Nicholas shows a clear parallel with Santa Claus. It goes like this:

In Myra there lived a merchant* with three daughters. At one time he had been happily married and the family had been extremely rich, but a combination of bad luck, poor business decisions and, perhaps above everything else, the merchant's loss of focus on his work since the death of his wife had seen them fall upon hard times. Now they barely had enough money for food and heating, let alone the luxuries they had once taken for granted.

The merchant's daughters were all reaching adulthood and would soon be expected to marry. In actual fact, the eldest daughter had met a man that she loved and was extremely keen on marrying him.† Her suitor felt the exact same way and, were it not for one obstacle, they could have been married and lived happily ever after. The obstacle was this: custom demanded that the bride's‡ father make a dowry payment to the would-be husband and his family. Such payments used to be – and in some places still are – a common part of wedding arrangements, and the dowry would be used both in order to fund the husband and wife in

* St Nicholas would later become the patron saint of merchants.
† St Nicholas would also become the patron saint of women who wished to marry.
‡ And the patron saint of brides.

setting up a new home together and also as a measure of status to prove that the bride was from a 'good' family from an acceptable social stratum. Unfortunately, with his finances as they were, it was absolutely impossible for the merchant to afford the dowry. Without it, the wedding could not take place.

Nowadays this sounds like a fairly trivial concern and no real barrier to happiness, but back then the consequences of this would have been severe. The family would have pressurised the husband-to-be to marry somebody else instead, and without a dowry it was unlikely that the girl would find another husband, even if she'd wanted to. If a woman remained unmarried* she would ultimately need to find a way to support herself without a husband's help. Given there were no career options available for women at this time, this meant her only option was to make a living by selling her body. This left the merchant with two choices: miraculously find a way to fund the dowry or condemn his beloved daughter to a lifetime of prostitution.†

The merchant was a Christian and the following Sunday he went to his church in Myra and prayed to God for a miraculous intervention. Nicholas overheard him and decided that the Christian thing to do would be to save the man from despair and the girl from sin by paying for the dowry himself. Nicholas, if you remember, was an orphan of wealthy parents who was committed to giving all of his money away to good causes (although presumably the fact that he still had money to give away means he had not rid himself of all

---

* Yep. St Nicholas is also the patron saint of unmarried women.
† You've guessed it – he's the patron saint of prostitutes too.

his worldly possessions, as Michael the Archimandrite had claimed . . .)

So that night, which just so happened to be the night before 6 December – subsequently given as Nicholas's saint's day, as it was the date of his death – he crept to the merchant's house and pushed a purse of gold through the window and onto the eldest daughter's windowsill. When the girl woke up the following morning, she was delighted to discover that her dowry had mysteriously appeared overnight and she was thus free to marry. She did so shortly afterwards and, although it is not recorded, I am sure that they lived happily ever after.

The merchant was very happy too. He was delighted by his miracle and pleased to see that his faith in God had been so generously rewarded. However, his joy lasted only a year before he discovered his middle daughter to be in the exact same predicament. She too was of marrying age and wildly in love, but she too needed a dowry for the wedding to go ahead. The merchant's business fortunes had not improved and once again he could not afford to pay what was needed. Following his previous success, he decided to once again go to the church and pray for a miracle. And once again Nicholas duly obliged by depositing a purse of gold on the middle daughter's windowsill on the evening of 5 December. Once again the daughter woke up to a joyful discovery and was free to enjoy matrimonial happiness.

The merchant was delighted at this second stroke of fortune. Nonetheless, for all his professed faith, he was a bit sceptical about the idea that God was really intervening on his behalf and was beginning to suspect it was likely to be a human hand, rather than divine intervention, that was appearing in his hour of need. Whatever the truth, the merchant was determined to find out who was behind these gifts so he could thank them and, no matter how many years it took, restore his pride by paying the money back.

This noble intention was all very well but did not change the fact that his financial situation still had not improved when, a year later, his youngest daughter came of age and wished to marry. Much like her elder sisters, the daughter had fallen in love with a wonderful hunk who was utterly besotted with her and, once again, the only obstacle was the absence of a dowry.

Initially at least, the merchant followed the same path as before. He went to the church and prayed for divine-intervention, then went home hoping he had done enough for his miracle to happen. This time, however, he was ready for the midnight visitor. He did not go to bed on the eve of 6 December but instead hid in the shadows of the trees and observed his youngest daughter's window, eagerly waiting to find out who would show up clutching the purse of gold.

The merchant might have been clever but Nicholas was cleverer still. He anticipated that the man would be lying in wait and, rather than approaching the daughter's window, he snuck across to the far side of the house and – taking care to stay out of the merchant's view – climbed up onto the roof. The merchant's eyes were so focused on his daughter's window that he failed to spot a bishop clambering towards his chimney. Nicholas dropped the purse of gold down the chimney and towards the fireplace, trusting in God that the money would be found in the morning.

It just so happened that the youngest daughter had washed her stockings the previous night and had hung them up to dry over the fire. The purse landed in the stockings and the girl found it there the following day. Like her sisters, she was absolutely delighted with both her find and the prospect of wedded bliss it brought her.

The merchant never did find out who had helped his daughters but came to accept that, one way or another, it had been an intervention from God. He became much more devout in his worship and lived a happy life. His business prospects also gradually improved, and he came to enjoy a comfortable life.

More euphemistic versions of this story tend to refer to the women as facing a lifetime of slavery rather than prostitution – stories about St Nicholas are often told to very young children and, as we're socially more comfortable with the idea of people being forced into servitude than we are with them having sex, the substitution of slavery saves parents from a multitude of embarrassing questions.

A more sinister variation presents the father as a questionable character. There are no dowries or husbands but instead the merchant actively wants to sell his daughters into prostitution simply because he is too lazy to work and wants to live off the earnings. St Nicholas intervenes by providing the daughters with money so they can give it to their father to avoid being pimped out. Fortunately, the money sates the man's greed and the merchant – bizarrely for a man who has got exactly what he wants for minimal effort and has just been rewarded for his unsavoury intentions – repents his actions and commits himself to Christianity.

Whichever version you go along with, this story contains some of the first roots of the idea of Santa Claus. We have the idea of anonymous gifts, the ritual of those gifts being given on a special date – in many European countries St Nicholas's Eve is still the main day for present-giving – and the significance of the presents arriving down the chimney and winding up in a stocking.

In reality, much of this is embellishment after the event. Michael the Archimandrite only tells of the coins being thrown through the window. The chimney and the stocking are later inventions used to retrospectively tighten the links between the St Nicholas and Santa Claus. But nonetheless we have our first anonymous Christmas gift-giver and, as such, the first seeds of the man who would be Santa Claus.

The Patron Saint of Sailors

St Nicholas's association with Christmas was not only due to the strengths of the myths. It was also about being in the right place at the right time. A lot of the midwinter mythology of the Middle Ages started to develop as Christianity mingled with paganism in the eleventh and twelfth centuries. The most influential power in Europe at the time was the Normans, who had descended from the Vikings and gradually expanded their influence across Europe. The seafaring roots of the Normans led them to seek out and adopt a figurehead with an affinity with sailors. And it turned out St Nicholas was the ideal man for the job.

Myra was a coastal city and a key port of the Roman Empire (St Paul was said to have changed ships at Myra when travelling to Rome from Jerusalem following his arrest in AD 61), and many of the myths about St Nicholas closely link him to the sea.

Stories abound of him saving sailors in storms – usually by using his mystical powers to calm stormy seas, but there are also tales of him walking on water to reach drowning sailors and, on one occasion, even using prayer to restore to life a sailor who died in a fall from a ship's mast.

St Nicholas didn't only prevent storms – occasionally he created them. One story tells of how an evil ship's captain plotted to extort money from the people of Myra by kidnapping their popular bishop and claiming a ransom. The captain duly lured Nicholas onto his boat, restrained him and sailed out of Myra, only for the bishop to cunningly whip up a fierce wind that drove the ship all the way back to the port. When the wind blew the ship into dock Nicholas calmly stood up and walked away unscathed as the captain and his men, all too awestruck and confused to react, simply stood and gawked at him. St Nicholas's reputation for mastery of the sea was so great that Nicholas became the patron saint of sailors.

St Nicholas Goes East

It was through this role that Nicholas's popularity as a saint grew. In the eighth and ninth centuries Myra was under threat of invasion from a new and rapidly expanding Slavic state called Rus.* The Byzantine Empire – which controlled Myra at the time – decided the best way to neutralize this new enemy was to attempt to befriend it by converting its people to Christianity.

In order to do this, Byzantine missionaries needed to sell the religion to the leaders of Rus, and that required a figurehead

* This, of course, would eventually become Russia.

33

with whom those leaders could connect. Unlike the population they ruled over, the Russian leaders were not Slavs but Normans descended from Vikings. The seafaring ways of the Normans' forefathers meant that, to the missionaries, a patron saint of sailors seemed the perfect salesman. So the missionaries used the tales of St Nicholas's affinity with seamen and his power over the sea as their way of selling Christianity to the Russian leaders. This ploy proved extremely successful. The Normans adopted St Nicholas as their favourite saint and spread his name everywhere they went. To this day, St Nicholas remains the patron saint of Russia, and the Normans would later play a huge role in championing Nicholas in western Europe too.

There was also an unexpected side effect. The Russian leaders then needed a way to sell the new religion to the peasant classes, most of whom were agricultural workers with no real link to or interest in stories of the sea. St Nicholas was therefore ascribed new qualities, apparently more based on convenience than any existing stories of the old bishop. He became a figurehead to farmers, a friend to shepherds and a companion to lonely mountain-dwellers. He was said to defend villages from fierce animals and, so great was his popularity, later his name was even invoked by peasants seeking protection from the tyranny of the Tsars.

As the years went on and his reputation spread, St Nicholas tended to be made the patron saint of rather a lot of things. In fact, the list of places, causes and groups for which St Nicholas has been declared patron saint is exhaustive and exhausting. It's also frequently contradictory including, for example, both judges and murderers, both students and teachers, and both oil traders and the poor. Perhaps he's at his most versatile when it comes to relationships – he's the patron saint of brides, grooms, unmarried men, unmarried women, lovers, virgins and women desirous of marrying. Or, in short, the patron saint of virtually everyone!

Incidentally, this flexibility has become a common theme in the story of St Nicholas and his personality has frequently been retrospectively altered as one group or another adopts him as their patron saint. Because so little was fixed about St Nicholas, he could easily be integrated into existing myths and presented as whatever his admirers wanted him to be. Santa Claus also demonstrates this malleability and much of his success and resonance has come from his ability to be all things to all people.

St Nicholas of Bari

Although his popularity steadily grew in Russia and eastern Europe in the years after his death, St Nicholas remained a minor figure in the West. He was certainly known to Christians, and his popularity and appeal was sufficient for people to make pilgrimages to Myra to see his remains, but his reputation in western Europe was in no way comparable to his vast popularity in Russia. The events that changed all that and began the process that made St Nicholas a key part of Christmas history lie in a story of graverobbing, the concealment of body parts and a vast papal squabble.

By the eleventh century religious tourism was becoming more and more popular in parts of Europe. In Italy in particular it was becoming increasingly clear that the way to encourage tourist traffic to a town was to have the remains of a saint buried within its walls.

This presented something of a problem to merchants in the town of Bari. They wanted to make money from tourism, but there was no saint buried nearby, and it seemed a bit optimistic and time-consuming to sit around and hope that someone local would die and that their deeds would be sufficient to ensure canonisation. So they decided to take a more proactive approach and simply steal the remains of a saint from somewhere else and, on 9 May 1087, they did exactly that. Sailors from Bari arrived in Myra to steal St Nicholas's remains and, to use a popular Christian euphemism of the time, translate them to Bari.

Accounts vary slightly in how exactly this was achieved. This was around the time that the Byzantine Empire was losing power to the Seljuq Turkish Empire, and there was a growing possibility that Myra might become part of Turkey and, in doing so, pass from Christian to Muslim hands. The merchants, who had initially arrived in Myra posing as pilgrims, claimed to have convinced the monks of Myra that the threat of invasion from Muslims was so great that they should hand over the remains (or relics) in order to preserve them. The monks disputed this account and it seems more likely that either bribery was involved or the merchants simply stole the remains.

The story does not end there. Legend has it that as the merchants tried to sail back to Italy the wind blew so hard that they found themselves unable to leave, as they were simply being blown straight back into port. The superstitious sailors initially regarded this as a sign that St Nicholas did not want to leave but then decided that the fault lay with one or two of the sailors who had, apparently for good luck, stolen some extra bones entirely unrelated to St Nicholas. The bones were duly returned and the ship was able to sail out of port and back to Bari.

However, this is not quite the end of the story either. When the merchants arrived in Bari there was an enormous dispute over whether the remains should be buried in the cathedral or the monastery. Today a dispute of this nature might result in a few huffy letters being published in a local newspaper, but in eleventh-century Italy it led to a full-blown riot after the Archbishop of Bari marched to the monastery to try to steal the bones back. Three people died and things got so bad that the Pope intervened. It was eventually agreed that a new basilica would be specially erected and the bones would be stored there.

Bizarrely, the story doesn't even end there. Bari wasn't the only Italian city interested in procuring a saint's bones. At the time of the theft, Venice had also been considering doing precisely the same thing (some accounts suggest a Venetian ship was already en route to Myra, only to learn that Bari had got there first). In what might be one of the strangest cases of sour grapes of all time, the Venetian authorities insisted that they too had inspected the grave and found that the sailors from Bari had carelessly left behind nearly a quarter of St Nicholas's bones, which Venice had now claimed for themselves. On this basis, the Venetians asserted that *they* had St Nicholas. And subsequent claims suggest that both the Barian and Venetian teams were rather hopeless, as both a church in Bucharest and a monastery in Athens claim to have Nicholas's right hand, whilst multiple other locations also claim to display some of the saint's bones.

But perhaps they are all wrong. Residents of Demre – the town in Turkey that stands where Myra once did – claim that their forefathers tricked all the aspiring grave-robbers and that Demre still has the bones of St Nicholas buried in its churchyard!

Whatever the truth, and however unethical robbing saints' graves might be, Bari's move was a commercial success and the basilica remains hugely popular as both a religious pilgrimage

37

site and a tourist attraction right up to this day. The move to the basilica (and his subsequent rebranding as St Nicholas of Bari) ultimately turned this minor saint into a hugely popular figure around Europe and, through European colonial expansion in later centuries, right across the whole world. What's more, it initiated a chain of events that within 300 years led to the first appearances of a man in robes and a white beard giving out presents to children, and the seeds of Santa Claus were sown.

2

Judgement Day

Sinterklaas (the Netherlands)

So far we have talked about St Nicholas as someone who was heroic. He saved sailors from storms, raised the dead, stopped children being cannibalised and protected women from prostitution. All in all, it's easy to see why people were so keen to sanctify him. But some legends show a different side – a severe, fierce and dogmatic man who was not afraid to back up his religious convictions with physical force when necessary. Interestingly, despite his reputation as a saviour of children, it was a very different side of his reputation that was most reflected when he first began to visit families at Christmas.

One example of Nicholas's violent commitment to his beliefs comes in a story of his attendance at the Council of Nicaea in AD 325, an early attempt by the Church to address religious differences that had grown among its clergy as Christianity spread across Europe. Picture the scene: a great hall, perhaps a bit like the grandiose halls in the Vatican where bishops and cardinals convene today. As the clergy gathered in their robes and earnestly discussed theology, Nicholas and another bishop called Arius argued over a crucial point of early Christian doctrine – specifically, whether Jesus Christ and God were part of one and the same essence (as Catholics and Protestants still believe) or whether Jesus was God's creation. Arius believed the latter. Nicholas believed the former. Arguments raged back and forth and their colleagues watched as the debate grew fiercer and fiercer. Eventually Nicholas decided to settle the matter once and for all and delivered a knockout blow to Arius's arguments. And when I say knockout blow, that is to say that he literally punched Arius in the face with such force that the dissenting bishop was knocked out cold and, by default, was in no position to continue the discussion.

The other bishops were at first rather unimpressed by this and promptly stripped Nicholas of his bishop's robes, chained him up and locked him in a cell. They also sacked him from his job as Bishop of Myra, which seemed a reasonable enough measure. A sacking is probably no less than most of us could expect for laying a colleague out cold during a heated work discussion.

It is said that as Nicholas lay in his cell that night he was visited by apparitions of Jesus and Mary, who thanked him for his commitment and gave him a new set of robes to wear. The next day his jailers walked in to find him freed from his chains, back in his bishop's clothing and sat patiently – and perhaps a bit smugly – waiting for them to arrive. His colleagues were so spooked by this unexpected intervention that they concluded at once that Jesus actually condoned this particular act of violence in his name. Nicholas was reinstated and not only was he readmitted to the debate but the rest of the Council immediately decided that he was completely right on this point of theology, and the Arius doctrine has been rejected ever since.

Even the small matter of death was not enough to stop Nicholas from wreaking violent revenge on those who did not show him sufficient respect. Sometime around the eleventh or twelfth century, a group of monks in the Netherlands had requested the church sing the responses of St Nicholas during their service. When the abbot refused, claiming that the responses were not sufficiently holy to warrant inclusion in a conventional church service, St Nicholas – who was naturally listening from Heaven – took it rather badly.

In fact, he was so aggrieved at the insolence of the abbot that he decided to descend from the heavens to pay him a visit. Many legends of St Nicholas praise the saint for his patience, tolerance and powers of persuasion, but in this particular story he took a rather different tack. Instead of trying to persuade the abbot by reason, he instead dragged him from his bed by his hair, pulled him out on the street and proceeded to heavily beat the abbot with a birch rod. Battered, bloody and probably rather astonished at being beaten up by a dead saint, the abbot begged for his life. St Nicholas agreed to spare him and, not surprisingly, the next day the abbot announced that he had changed his mind about the music. This sort of behaviour is a world away from the modern Santa Claus. It is also a very different St Nicholas to the one the Greeks or Russians were accustomed to – not so much a protector from tyranny but rather the actual embodiment of it.

A Brief and Bloody History of Medieval Bari

St Nicholas might have had a reputation for mythical violence but, during his first three centuries in Bari, the human violence that surrounded his bones was all too real. His remains arrived at a time when the Normans and the Byzantines were squabbling over possession of the city. War after war was fought and control repeatedly passed between the rival empires. In 1117 the Archbishop of Bari was murdered, and in 1146 Norman warriors razed much of the city to the ground. Many modern tourist guides claim this destruction was at the hands of the brilliantly named William the Evil. Sadly, it is hard to independently verify whether a Norman raider with such a stereotypically super-villainous moniker really existed, but certainly the destruction itself was an actual historical fact and an event that would be repeated several times over the next 200 years. Luckily for Nicholas and his devotees, however, the basilica was unharmed and his remains untouched.

The violent times into which Nicholas's myth was born in western Europe were further compounded by the beginning of the Crusades. The politics of how the Crusades started are long and complex but basically the Byzantine Empire – essentially the last remnants of the Eastern Roman Empire – got tired of simultaneously fighting the Seljuq Turks to the east and the Normans to the west. They decided the best way to defend themselves was to approach Pope Urban II and request assistance in whipping up the Norman Empire into a frenzy over the threat to Christianity from the Muslim forces of the east and, by doing so, unite with the Normans and other European Christian nations in a 'holy' war against this common enemy.

For the next three centuries, Bari was a key port for Christians heading east to forcibly spread their message. Religious tourism had already been growing in popularity before the Crusades – this was, of course, Bari's motivation for stealing Nicholas's remains in the first place. What's more, the fact that Seljuq Turks kept attacking Christian pilgrims in the Holy Land was a major reason why other nations were so keen to join the Byzantine quest – but the Crusades pushed travel and tourism (and violence and bloodshed, for that matter) up to a whole new level. St Nicholas was one of the saints who profited the most from this. Christians returning from fighting the Crusades would often visit the basilica, and many of the Christian warriors adopted him as both a good-luck charm and their own personal saint. As a result, the legends of St Nicholas were transported across medieval Europe. Towns such as Amsterdam, Amiens and Ghent adopted him as their patron saint, and thousands of churches dedicated to St Nicholas sprang up all across Europe. It was in these churches – and against a backdrop of this violently evangelical form of Christianity – that the first stirrings of St Nicholas, the Christmas visitor, began.

The Rise of Sinterklaas

It is hard to trace exactly where the tradition of gift-giving on St Nicholas's day began, but during the twelfth century nuns in central France began to creep out on St Nicholas's Eve to leave anonymous gifts of food and drink at the homes of the poor, possibly in recognition of Nicholas's own reputation for giving presents anonymously. The tradition spread across Europe over the next century or so.

By the fourteenth century a tradition had begun at Church schools affiliated with St Nicholas where, on 6 December, a teacher would dress as St Nicholas and pass judgement on the pupils' work over the previous year. If the pupil was good, the teacher would honour the memory of St Nicholas by rewarding the good child with pocket money or sweets in recognition of the saint's reputation for rewarding the deserving. If the pupil was bad, the teacher would honour the memory of St Nicholas by punishing the miscreant with a beating with a birch rod in recognition of the saint's other reputation for doling out physical violence to his enemies. Over the next century this tradition of judgement, reward and punishment would spread to households too, with similar rituals of an annual visit from St Nicholas.

Traditions of St Nick visiting households happened right across Europe, stretching from Romania in the east to Spain in the west and France and the Lowlands in the north. Switzerland, Germany, Austria, Luxembourg and the Balkans all have strong traditions involving St Nicholas, but perhaps the most quintessential and influential version is that of the Dutch Sinterklaas.

A Visit from St Nicholas

As the description of the teacher in the Church school suggests, the St Nicholas of the Middle Ages was a world away from the kindly protector and saviour of children, sailors and farmers, and further still from the idea of the modern Santa Claus. The St Nicholas who visited might have been inspired by the story of the man who left money for the merchant and his three young daughters to save them from a lifetime of cruelty and prostitution, but it was the violent dogmatist that he was based on: the St Nicholas who punched out bishops who dared to disagree with him and who came down from Heaven to beat the living daylights out of abbots who did not deem him sufficiently holy; St Nicholas as an agent of divine retribution.

St Nicholas – or Sinterklaas as the Dutch call him – would arrive at households on 5 December, the eve of St Nicholas's Day, and test children on their knowledge of scripture. Prior to his visit, children would try to memorise the Bible for hours in their desperation to pass the tests he would set them. And for good reason – passing the test might mean being rewarded with sweets and treats, but failure could cost them their soul. Nowadays a visit to Santa Claus is a wonderful and magical experience where they meet a jolly, warm, friendly character who sits children on his knee,[*] jovially asks if they have been naughty or nice and merrily gives them a Christmas present, chuckling all the time. In contrast, the Sinterklaas of the Dutch Middle Ages was a severe, threatening religious autocrat who preached fire and brimstone, judged children's moral characters and threatened to damn them all to a lifetime in Hell. If children looked forward to his visits at all – and I'm not at all convinced any of them did – their anticipation was mixed with a sense of fear and trepidation. This was a dress rehearsal for the day of judgement.

The ritual of the visit would go as follows:

A few minutes before he was due to arrive, children would sing a song welcoming St Nicholas and – presumably without a trace of irony – praising his benevolence and kindness. At the crucial moment sweets would be thrown through the door. No sooner had they landed on the floor than the door would open and Sinterklaas would arrive.

Usually portrayed by a family member, friend or neighbour, Sinterklaas was an austere, harsh-looking man clad in white bishop's robes. He would normally be an old man (for bishops usually were) and often had grey hair and a beard (for bishops usually did) – but he was certainly not the jolly, cheerful figure we imagine today (indeed, bishops of the time probably weren't). Rather than carrying his now-traditional sack of presents, he would clutch a birch rod and wave it menacingly – a clear reminder to the children that the ghostly violence he administered to abbots whose musical selections he disagreed with could just as easily be meted out to them.

Sinterklaas would glare at the nervous children and, unsmiling,

* Child safeguarding issues permitting.

demand answers to questions on the Bible. Which sea did Moses part? Who was turned into a pillar of salt? Which saint was converted on the road to Damascus? On which mountain did God give Moses the Ten Commandments? To which holy figure did John 1:8 refer?*

If children knew the answers they would be handed sweets and warned to ensure they remained good for the following year. If children got a few questions wrong they would be soundly beaten. But if they had failed to learn anything at all they would be dragged off to Hell.

To understand the terror this instilled in children, it is important to remember that this was a time when Hell and eternal damnation were seen as very real threats for anyone who was not sufficiently pious, and the role of a bishop or priest involved ensuring their flock was so terrified of the possibility of an after-life of eternal torment that they would obey the Church without question. The visit of St Nicholas was an early test of a child's devotion to the Lord, and every child was terrified of failing. Without his favour and protection, there was nothing to stop the devil taking them away. Children really, really did need to be good for goodness' sake.

Being threatened by a vengeful bishop preaching fire and brimstone must surely have been a horrific experience for any child. However, the whole thing was made significantly worse by the fact that Sinterklaas had no need to carry out his threats or punishments himself, for the Devil actually accompanied Sinterklaas on his travels. He came in the form of a terrifying, primeval-looking servant. He was clad in rattling chains to

* For anyone who wanted to test themselves: the Red Sea; the wife of Lot; Paul the Apostle; Mount Sinai; John the Baptist.

emphasise St Nicholas's power over him. He brandished a huge stick ready to beat naughty children with. Worse still, he carried a big burlap sack just in case he had to spirit a child off to Hell. In Dutch folklore his name was Zwarte Piet or Black Peter.

Black Peter

To some, Black Peter was simply a brutal Moorish servant that St Nicholas had acquired. To others, he was Satan himself, who had been captured and subjugated by St Nicholas and compelled to do his bidding. Either way, what was certain was that he was both vicious and single-minded in his determination to punish misbehaving children. A beating from Black Peter was said to be far more severe and brutal than any discipline the child had ever received before. If a child sufficiently angered St Nicholas for him to demand that Black Peter take the child away in his sack, then the child would be trapped in Hell for an entire year, only getting the chance to repent the following Christmas. Make no mistake – Black Peter ensured that the consequences of getting a wrong answer in one of St Nicholas's tests were terrifying beyond words.

Like Sinterklaas, Zwarte Piet would usually be played by a local person dressed up in costume, a costume which is now one of the most controversial aspects of Dutch Christmas folklore. Early depictions of Black Peter saw performers portray him by blacking their hands and faces with soot. This is certainly politically incorrect and a bit tasteless by modern standards. However – if you accept the idea of Black Peter being the Devil rather than a Moorish servant – the similarities to the image of someone 'blacking up' could be dismissed as an unfortunate coincidence. After all, the modern idea of the Devil as a bright-red creature with horns and a tail is relatively recent. In the Middle Ages there was no universally accepted idea of what the Devil looked like, but he was often depicted as being black in colour, perhaps because he was perceived as an evil figure strongly associated with shadows and darkness.

However, this explanation is complicated by the fact that Black Peter was said to originate from Spain – a country that had only just recovered its territory from the African Caliphate that had controlled much of the Iberian Peninsula from the tenth century onwards – and his depiction as black could have been rooted in hostility to the country's former rulers. And of course the Crusades were a time when Europe's non-white Muslim opponents were literally presented as being anti-Christ.

The nineteenth century saw a change in how Black Peter was portrayed. This was when Christmas experienced a major renaissance during which many medieval traditions were reinvented with a modern twist. It was also the height of colonialism, and centuries of slave trading had meant non-white people were seen as inferior to Europeans, perhaps even less than human, and certainly ripe for mocking and satire. The person playing Black Peter began to take things a bit further and created the image that largely remains to this day. Not only would the performer blacken all visible skin but he also donned pink lipstick and an Afro wig and wore garish jewellery. His behaviour and demeanour were fierce and primal and he was presented as a violent 'untamed savage', bound up with chains and clearly subservient to St Nicholas, his dominant 'master'. Until very recently, he would also speak Pidgin Dutch with a strong mock-Surinamese accent. All this considered, it is unsurprising that the depiction of Black Peter causes offence to many people and is a source of controversy and bemusement to people outside the Netherlands.

Critics of the character argue that such an overtly racial image is a throwback to the days of slavery and colonialism. They believe the clear stereotyping in Black Peter's appearance can only be a symbol of racism which both offends and excludes the black population that makes up a sizable part of the country today. His defenders insist that he is merely a representation of the Devil and that the parallels to offensive racial caricatures are a combination of unlucky chance and the sensitivities of over-zealous advocates of modern political correctness. Furthermore, Black Peter is a key part of Dutch heritage and national identity and many Dutch people can be rather sensitive and defensive when non-Dutch observers criticise their traditions and culture.

Many modern-day Dutch people are keen to preserve the tra-dition of Zwarte Piet and insist that they are preserving existing traditions rather than attempting to cause racial offence, explain-ing that the character is black because he is covered in soot from climbing up and down chimneys. However, it is very difficult to disassociate his appearance from similar racial caricatures such as minstrels and golliwogs, and it is extremely hard to believe prejudice played no part in how his image was created in the nineteenth century.

In 2011 the former Dutch colony of Suriname banned depic-tions of Zwarte Piet in public, and the same year Amsterdam city councillor Andrée Van Es became the first high-profile politician to publicly denounce the character. Attempts have also been made to portray Peter in different-coloured make-up such as blue, green and yellow. Nonetheless, the traditions have proved hard to shake off. Van Es was heavily criticised by Dutch tradi-tionalists, and an experiment by Dutch public broadcasters NPS to portray a rainbow-coloured Peter lasted only a year before he reverted to his blackface origins. Meanwhile, the Dutch community in Vancouver were so vexed by the controversy over their use of Zwarte Piet in their annual Christmas celebrations in 2011 that local authorities decided to cancel them entirely, rather than make the decision to phase out the character. For now, however, Peter still appears in his blackface guise to play a major part in Christmas celebrations in the Netherlands itself.

The Modern-Day Sinterklaas

The precise ritual around the arrival of Sinterklaas differed from town to town and has changed through the ages, but the Netherlands has held on to its traditions more than many other countries in the face of the rising global popularity of Santa Claus. Modern celebrations therefore provide a useful window into the historical traditions surrounding the character.

Whilst many other countries have seen gift-giving traditions shift to Christmas Day, Sinterklaas still delivers gifts in the Netherlands on 5 December, the eve of his annual feast day. Unlike Santa Claus's propensity for sneaking around at night, St Nicholas arrives in the Netherlands in full public view a few weeks before 6 December. He does not use a sleigh but instead arrives on a steamboat, accompanied by Black Peter, from his home in Spain. The fact that the Dutch think a Greek bishop who hails from what is now Turkey and is buried in south Italy actually originates from Spain might initially seem confusing, but the reason for this is political. During the fifteenth and sixteenth centuries, when the mythology around Sinterklaas really took shape, the Netherlands was under Spanish rule – these were the days when kings tended to marry for territorial conquest and diplomacy rather than love, and a series of marriages of convenience meant that Spanish kings gained more and more Dutch territory. As a means of controlling power and preventing rebellion, the Spanish rulers tended to appoint fellow Spaniards rather than Dutch people to positions of authority, so virtually all powerful and influential figures in the Netherlands were Spanish. This included bishops. As all Dutch bishops were, in fact, Spanish bishops, it made sense to the Dutch that St Nicholas should be Spanish too.

Sinterklaas's arrival in the middle of November is now a major national event. A different coastal town is chosen each year and the event is broadcast live on television. A huge crowd will gather prior to his arrival and the town mayor will be waiting on the quay with a host of red-coated musketeers. Eventually Sinterklaas will arrive, clad in full bishop's robes and cape and clutching a mitre. Black Peter accompanies him, but now acts more as an administrator than an instrument of violence – his main role is keeping a ledger recording good and bad conduct by local children. The mayor greets him and gives a short speech and then Sinterklaas goes on a politician-style choreographed walkabout where he will shake some hands, greet some children and ask some questions about their behaviour – albeit in a far more jovial and less fearsome manner than his counterpart from the Middle Ages.

All the while a brass band plays traditional Dutch Christmas songs and eventually Sinterklaas leaps on a white horse and leads the mayor, the band and numerous other revellers on a procession through the city.

It is at this point that the distinction between Sinterklaas and Santa Claus starts to disappear as Sinterklaas and Peter spend the next few weeks making public appearances in schools, hospitals, shopping centres and restaurants. The ritual is a familiar one to anyone who has been to see Santa as a child. Sinterklaas listens to children's accounts of good and bad behaviour, and Peter takes a similar role to the elf, handing out the gifts to children (so long as they have been good). He still punishes the bad but no longer beats children himself, instead giving naughty children a stick to pass on to their parents so they can beat the child should they choose to do so. One tradition that does remain is that he still carries his sack to spirit away children who really misbehave, although he now takes them to Spain rather than to Hell – a much more appealing prospect, despite the worst excesses of British holidaymakers!

Sinterklaas's nocturnal activities have a familiar ring to them. His white horse can fly over rooftops and, in the weeks between his arrival and 5 December, Sinterklaas and Black Peter hover over Holland's chimneys so that Peter can overhear children's conversations and judge if they have been naughty or nice. On 5 December itself children leave a clog by the fire. It is Black Peter rather than Sinterklaas that climbs down the chimneys to fill the clogs with sweets.

The evening of 5 December is also when adults will exchange gifts. Families and older children will receive one gift each, traditionally drawing names from a hat to decide who each person is buying for. A key part of this tradition is that the present must also contain a poem, said to be from Sinterklaas himself, which is designed to embarrass the recipient. The usual way of doing this is by referring to a toe-curling incident that has taken place during the year but, especially when giving gifts to teenagers, it might instead refer to a secret crush.

After 6 December St Nicholas secretly slips out of the country without ritual and makes his way back to Spain. A few weeks later, Christmas Day is a much quieter occasion, with a family meal and perhaps a church service. Traditionally, further presents are not exchanged on Christmas Day.

Nonetheless, despite Dutch adherence to its traditional celebrations, there has been a growing custom of Christmas gifts being given on Christmas Day rather than St Nicholas's Day (especially once children get too old to believe in Sinterklaas). Also, some families now have a tradition of Sinterklaas being followed a few weeks later by the arrival of Christmas Man – who looks remarkably like Santa Claus – from Finland on Christmas Eve to deliver more presents. The gradual process of Santa Claus taking the place of traditional celebrations is a familiar theme repeated elsewhere across Europe over the twentieth century. But for now, at least, Sinterklaas still reigns supreme over Dutch Christmas celebrations and, for better or worse, Black Peter remains at his side.

Santa's Evil Helpers

The Krampus (Austria, Germany, Hungary and Croatia)

The peculiar traditions of Zwarte Piet might seem strange to outsiders, but the idea of St Nicholas being accompanied by a fierce devil-like creature who administered brutal punishments to naughty children was a common feature of Christmas celebrations across Europe.

German children were visited by Knecht Ruprecht, Belsnickel, Hans Muff or Klaubauf; French children by Rubbels or Père Fouettard. Swiss children feared a visit by Schmutzli whilst, to the Czechs and the Slovaks, Nicholas's companion was literally the Devil himself. Meanwhile, areas around the Alps, and especially Austria, had the Krampus. These figures tended to be local to certain parts of their host countries and all played a similar role to Zwarte Piet: accompanying St Nicholas on his visits to children's homes and terrifying them by divining whether they had been good or bad; then, if they had been bad, meting out punishments that varied from 'merely' giving them a fierce beating to spiriting them away either to Hell or to a certain death.

Not only did these characters play similar roles in Christmas celebrations but they frequently shared a similarity of appearance. They would generally dress in furs, perhaps with skin blackened with soot, had goat horns and long pink tongues, essentially representing something between a Neanderthal man, a satyr and a devil. Which of those three figures they resembled most closely might change but the general image remained largely the same.

These similarities can cause problems in understanding the

origins of the characters, and it is very easy to fall into the trap of conflating them and assuming them to all be the exact same character under different names. This is complicated even further by the fact that the nature of oral traditions – and the tendency by storytellers to steal bits of one story to spice up another – meant that, even by the time writers like the Brothers Grimm first began to document oral folktales in the early nineteenth century, the characters had already begun to merge into one another. Factor in the local differences between even the original figures themselves and it can be near impossible to be certain where one character begins and another ends.

The Czech Devil

Nonetheless, the characters do have differences in both their appearance and history that make them distinct from one another. The depiction of the Devil who accompanies St Nicholas in the Czech Republic and Slovakia bears many similarities to the original devilish Zwarte Piet, but St Nicholas has a third companion too in the form of an angel. It is the angel who rewards the good children whilst the Devil punishes the bad, and St Nicholas stands aloof as an impartial judge.

Even today, the visit of Nicholas and his friends can be traumatic for children. Christmas traditions in most parts of Europe have now dispensed with the threat of dragging children off to Hell, but many Czechs still revel in it! The Devil will ask the child if they have behaved and then ask the parents the same question. If the child says they have behaved and the parents agree, then naturally all is fine and the child receives a treat. If the children admit to behaving badly then St Nicholas is fine with that too. He'll congratulate the child on his or her honesty and ask them to promise to behave better next year. However, if the child says they have behaved, and the parents say otherwise, then the child is the Devil's to punish. First of all, the Devil will shake his chains and threaten to throw the child in his sack. Sometimes, especially if there is a large group of children, the Devil will go somewhat further. He will physically seize the child and carry him or her off with him – often kicking and screaming – outside the room and out of view of the other children. For the next five minutes, the children will really believe the Devil has dragged their friend off to Hell.

Eventually, some time after the cries and sobs of distress have died down, the Devil returns with the child and they are given the chance to redeem themselves by singing a song in praise of St Nicholas. Should the child do so successfully, the angel will give them a present and the Devil will let them off with the warning that next time – NEXT time – they really will be taken to Hell.

Père Fouettard

Not all Nicholas's assistants are devils. France's Père Fouettard (literally the 'whipping father') is very human and he originates from a tale we have already encountered. For Père Fouettard is said to have once been an innkeeper in the town of Myra – an innkeeper who St Nicholas encountered once during his life as a miracle-working bishop. Indeed, he is said to be the very innkeeper who, during a great famine, lured three children to his inn with the promise of a meal, before murdering them, chopping them up and pickling them in a barrel ready to sell as food. When I told this story earlier, I mentioned that the innkeeper was overcome with remorse but neglected to add that he was so penitent he decided to dedicate his afterlife to St

Nicholas's service and now accompanies the saint around parts of eastern France, assisting him with his festive duties. Clearly the fact that, despite his remorse, St Nicholas has assigned him the task of terrifying naughty children shows Nicholas has a clear idea of where Fouettard's strengths lie. Certainly the presence of a cannibalistic murderer with a propensity for eating children – even a reformed cannibalistic murderer with a propensity for eating children – and a sadistic enthusiasm for punishing those who misbehave adds a certain *frisson* to Nicholas's visits and makes for a truly terrifying Christmas companion.

These days Père Fouettard, like Zwarte Piet, has become a much more benign figure and his days of brutal threats to beat or abduct misbehaving children are sadly long behind him. For a brief spell in the 1930s[5] he struck out on his own from St Nicholas, got married and re-emerged in America. Anglicised as Father Flog (and married to the like-minded Madame Flog), he emerged as a bogeyman who, in tandem with his wife, assisted parents of recalcitrant children by devising and carrying out gleefully malicious punishments for them. This resurgence came from an English translation of a French comic strip where naughty children were sadistically punished with sanctions that fitted the crime. Father Flog would cut the tongues off children who lied, lock little girls in cages for running about too much and imprison children who did not listen to their parents. Madame Flog would hide in saucepans of food to catch and administer justice to greedy children who ate too much. None of this had anything to do with Christmas, but similarities with Black Peter and the original Père Fouettard still remained – good children were given sweets instead of punishments and Father Flog carried a sack on his back to carry away anyone who misbehaved.

Belsnickel

Belsnickel – whose name comes from a combination of the name Nicholas and the German word for 'to wallop somebody' – could either be a very tall elf or a very short hermit. He dressed in the same outfit of rags, chains and soot as St Nicholas's assistants did but, unlike those assistants, he often carried out his activities on his own and acted as both the rewarder and the punisher – St Nicholas and his devil. True, he would still be the one who handed out the ridiculously brutal sentences, but he was a bringer of gifts and sweets too. In fact his elfin appearance and solitary, unpredictable behaviour have made US academic Phyllis Siefker question whether the anarchic, untamed 'wild man' Belsnickel, rather than the moral, upright St Nicholas, is the true genesis of Santa Claus.[6] In parts of Germany, Knecht Ruprecht and Hans Muff – very similar characters to Belsnickel, and perhaps even versions of the same figure – occasionally carry out a similar solo role. True, they do often accompany St Nicholas, but sometimes Christianity leaves the party entirely and the Devil takes control.

Schmutzli

The Swiss Schmutzli appeared in a variety of guises and was sometimes a supernatural devil and sometimes simply a very strong, simple-minded farmhand. His appearance varied too. On occasions, like Zwarte Piet, he would have a face blackened with soot. Alternatively, he could resemble a black-coated St Nicholas doppelgänger or sometimes an evil druid. Now and again he simply looked a bit like a psychotic hobo. Like many of his counterparts, he spent the Middle Ages accompanying St Nicholas and threatening to beat children or spirit them away.

However, as seems to be the case with these figures across Europe, he appears to have become more benign with age. Now the Schmutzli's main role is to appear at an event called the Klausjagen – a procession in honour of St Nicholas held in Switzerland every year. He still carries a stick and occasionally threatens to use it. But these days he does not beat anybody. His main role instead is handing out gingerbread and pastries to revellers. It's a humiliating comedown for a once terrifying character.

His bad influence has not waned entirely however – the Swiss Broadcasting Corporation's international service reported an incident in 2008 where, in the town of Lucerne, a group of teenage boys dressed up as Schmutzlis and terrorised younger boys, thrashing one poor soul with a broomstick.[7]

Granted, this behaviour sounds more than a little odd, but it is actually closer to the original roots of the character than you might think. Becoming Schmutzlis was originally a ritual for groups of young men to release pent-up aggression by dressing up, charging around and making a lot of noise. But there was another motive for Schmutzlis – it was essentially a marriage protection racket to 'defend' local women from outside suitors.[8] The logic went that men were less likely to approach a village to attempt to find a wife if they knew there were gangs of local men in terrifying costumes willing to beat them for seducing 'their' women. You might take a view on the ethics at play here but, so far as self-preservation goes, it's actually pretty infallible!

The Origins of Santa's Evil Helpers

Sadly, it is unclear whether any of the other helpers St Nicholas acquired sprang up due to young men wanting to limit sexual competition and purloin the most desirable local women for themselves, but certainly there are clear similarities between the characters. All of them accompany St Nicholas. All represent, if not the Devil and the forces of evil specifically, then something primal, wild and untamed. Furthermore, all of them take a gleefully sadistic pleasure in punishing young children. The same themes crop up over and over: beating children with a birch rod, smuggling naughty children away in a sack, dragging disobedient children to Hell ... the usual sort of thing. The characters may have developed with differences in their appearance and back-stories, but they clearly share the same roots.

The origins and the spread of folk tales are often hard to trace. Stories developed and were handed down from generation to generation. They travelled between communities when people mingled – perhaps through trade or when young people left their own kinship groups in order to find work or potential mates due to a dearth of available partners within their own areas. However, travel and communication were obviously much less structured than they are today and you would expect ideas, stories and customs to have taken longer to spread. The speed at which these evil helpers began to spring up over a relatively short period of time is therefore rather surprising.

Undoubtedly the Church was a hugely powerful organisation and it certainly would have played its part in spreading a uniform Christmas mythology around St Nicholas and his cruel companions, but this does not completely explain how these characters came into being. For one thing, there is no obvious root for these evil helpers within Christian mythology and no obvious motive for the Church to have created them. In fact the Church tended to tolerate – rather than encourage – such figures. It co-opted Schmutzli and associated him with St Nicholas because it wanted to tame the character and channel the rowdy behaviour of local youths into something more Christian. This was a pattern repeated across Europe through much of the Middle Ages. The Church spread Christianity by adopting and adapting existing mythologies and giving them Christian meanings, and it tolerated practices that were not strictly orthodox as long as it could pass them off as nominally 'Christian' by giving them a religious meaning.

What's more, the Church might not have had a huge appetite for these evil figures, but ordinary people certainly did. The traditions of Zwarte Piet, Knecht Ruprecht, Père Fouettard and Schmutzli were enthusiastically embraced by ordinary people. The way the characters caught on quickly over a vast area of Europe suggests they had their roots in ideas that existed long before St Nicholas started the audition process for potential assistants. In fact, the most likely source of these characters is within pagan rituals that existed before Christianity and were merged into the new religion by missionaries eager to convert locals to their religion.

To understand the origin of the characters, it is first important to remember the traditional belief, common across Europe, that midwinter was the time when ghosts, ghouls, demons and the undead were free to roam the Earth searching for souls to enslave or consume. Anyone unwise enough to wander out alone during the dark, cold, unforgiving winter nights was putting themselves in grave mortal and spiritual danger.

People therefore devised rituals and superstitions to keep themselves safe. One of these beliefs was in the idea of a god – or more often a goddess – who had the power and strength to protect people from the evil demons and ghouls that might otherwise get out of control and break into people's homes and kill them. A ritual began where people would dress up as the goddess and her servants and go from house to house driving the demons and evil souls away. The costumes these revellers wore tended to consist of furs and animal masks – usually an animal with horns to drive away these damned souls.

The goddess, however, was not a benign, unconditional protector of all; she would only save those who had behaved in ways that pleased her, thus proving themselves to be worthy of saving. If you did not perform the necessary rituals to appease her, she would not give you her protection and would become far worse than the demons and evil spirits you were seeking protection from. For the goddess was a chastiser as much as a protector, and she would punish those who did not respect her sufficiently in horrific ways. This goddess took different forms and different names across Europe, but her tradition is best preserved in the German, Italian and Austrian Alps in the form of a creature called Perchta.

Perchta

Perchta's appearance changed from region to region. In Tyrol, Frau Perchta appeared as a mischievous, dishevelled old woman. In other places her appearance could depend on how you perceived her and whether you had pleased her. If you were faithful, obedient and observed her rituals, Perchta would appear to you as a woman of divine beauty. If you angered her, she would appear as a demonic, horned monster with a ferocious bloodlust.

Her most common form of attack was to sneak into your house in the dead of night during the winter and creep up to the room where you were sleeping. The goddess would then take out a knife and, whilst you slept unaware, she would slit your stomach open and remove your innards and your intestines. She'd then replace those innards with pebbles and straw and sew you back up so whoever discovered your corpse the next morning would find absolutely no signs of physical damage. In the days before regular autopsies, nobody would ever prove that you had not simply and peacefully passed away in your sleep.

One protection against this grisly fate was to eat plenty of the cakes that were baked to celebrate Perchta's festival day (the eve of Twelfth Night). If you had eaten enough, her knife could not hurt you and would merely bounce off your skin. Indeed, eating the right food was the best defence against angering Perchta. It was very important to mark Perchta's Day by eating a traditional meal – either herring and dumplings or pancakes made from meal and milk, depending on the local area. Eating food in her honour pleased Perchta and, so long as you did so, you were virtually guaranteed protection. If you should eat anything else, however, Frau Perchta would again appear with her trusty knife to slit open your stomach (she clearly really enjoyed doing that), remove the offending food, replace it with straw and bricks and sew your stomach back up again. After you had eaten on Perchta's Day, it was important to leave the remains of the meal on the table so Perchta could gobble them up when she came to visit after you had gone to bed. However, it was equally important not to go back downstairs and try to spot her. Anyone who tried to spy on Frau Perchta as she went around the house would be blinded for the next year. The tradition of leaving food out for a nocturnal visitor and taking care not to try and spot them might put you in mind of a certain Christmas figure . . .

Up Jumped the Devil

The Christianity that replaced pagan religions had a very different view of good and evil from its predecessors. Pagan gods and goddesses such as Perchta were generally revered due to their being all-powerful rather than necessarily being 'good'. Certainly they rewarded the good and the faithful, but generally the value of obedience and fidelity to the most powerful figure around was placed above the value of moral or social good. You could say the same about the Old Testament, which introduces a god that is happy to punish disobedience by destroying cities, to virtually wipe out mankind with huge floods, to destroy world peace and global unity in order to maintain his power or to trick someone into thinking they have to murder their child to prove their devotion to the Lord[*]. Just as Perchta would punish those who disobeyed her, so the Hebrew god destroyed Sodom and Gomorrah on account of the levels of sin and caused a great flood to rid the world of people who did not have sufficient faith in him.

There are obviously reasons for this – in many cases early religions and beliefs were rituals developed for nomadic peoples in uncertain environments who might face physical danger unexpectedly and have to act suddenly. In times of crisis, obedience would be key and somebody breaking with the orders of the leader of the group could easily place lives in danger. Moreover, as social customs were being drawn up, autocratic leaders feared challenges to their leadership and the repercussions of struggles for power and authority were probably feared by all. It made

[*] Respectively, the stories of Sodom and Gomorrah, Noah and his ark, the Tower of Babel, and Abraham and Isaac.

sense to have religions where obedience was the highest virtue of all.

On the other hand, Christianity was actually born from the idea of a man – albeit a man who was really the Son of God – actively challenging and disobeying the most powerful people in the society. It matured in areas where it was a minority, persecuted religion, and by the time it finally achieved social respectability humans had generally evolved in established, settled and structured societies with less need for absolute obedience in the face of sudden dangers. Obedience was still very important, of course, but as there were rich and powerful people (and existing religious figures) who were not Christians, the obedience had to be channelled in the right direction.

Perhaps it was a need for Christianity to be seen as the one 'correct' religion, but God became not only a source of power but a force for good alone. Good things happened because of God and, if bad things happened, it was either a short-term negative consequence of the 'good' that God was trying to do in the long run or the result of the power wielded by dark forces outside of God's control. This made existing pagan figures like Perchta a problem – not just because she was being presented as having godlike powers but also because she represented good and evil within the same being, and as such confused the moral simplicity of a good 'God' against the forces of evil.

Early Christian missionaries knew pagan gods like Perchta were too ingrained in local customs to be eradicated entirely, but perhaps it was possible to play down the 'good' aspects, play up the 'bad' aspects and present them as the forces of evil that the 'good' God was working to combat. The images of people dressed as the pagan gods, with animal furs and horns, began to be seen as representations of the Devil and are the most likely forefathers of the horned, pointy-tailed Devil depicted in popular culture today. People who worshipped pagan gods were told they were actually worshipping the forces of evil; paganism became frowned upon and more and more people turned to Christianity.

Nonetheless, the actual ritual of dressing up as a 'wild man' or a pagan god and banishing evil was a popular local custom that people did not want to lose. Christians permitted it to continue but, just like the missionaries who first converted the leaders of Russia, they found a way to combine it with Christian beliefs. So instead of powerful, untamed figures they became the subservient companions of St Nicholas. They still had the power to implement evil and vengeance, but only under Nicholas's watchful eye. It is likely that Zwarte Piet, Knecht Ruprecht, Père Fouettard and the various other sinister assistants St Nicholas took with him around Europe all stem from this need to convert pagan gods into Christian figures.

Meanwhile, Perchta survived, but her story changed. Because Christian beliefs could not be reconciled with the idea of her as a goddess – and perhaps also because social conventions could not accept the idea of a woman in a position of power – she instead became a mere witch or a malevolent spirit. And she gradually changed from a protector (albeit an ambiguous one) from the demons that stalked the winter to actually becoming their personification. She would visit households during the twelve days of Christmas in order to observe festive preparations, paying attention to whether the festive meal had been prepared correctly (murdering anyone who did not have the traditional meal of the time – often fish and gruel) and to whether children and servants had done what they were told that year. A particular concern was whether young women had spun enough wool.

If the person in question had been good, they would be rewarded with a gold coin. If not, they could expect to have their belly split open by the angry spirit.

This truce and tolerance between pagan traditions and Christianity did not last forever. The witch trials, the Reformation and Puritanism all made attempts to 'purify' Christianity and rid it of all pagan practices. Dressing up as a devil, even for festive holidays, was seen as proof of witchcraft punishable by death in Austria during the Inquisition. The popularity of many of Nicholas's assistants – like Nicholas himself and Christmas in general – dwindled as a result. This meant that many of these devil characters disappeared, and those that were resurrected during the nineteenth-century renaissance of Christmas came back in a far milder form than before.

Traditions around Perchta survived better than most, largely due to a simple fact of geography. It was a tradition that had developed in Alpine countries where communities were far more remote, and it was much harder for central governments and religious authorities to have influence. The law might have banned her, but the chances of detection were so slim that Perchta could continue to be celebrated in relative safety. So too could another of the Alps' midwinter characters that I have so far only touched upon but who is perhaps the most marvellous of all Nicholas's evil assistants: the Krampus.

The Krampus

In many ways the Krampus is similar to what's gone before. Like Perchta, he had pagan roots and was originally said to ward off evil spirits. Like Zwarte Piet, Père Fouettard and the others, he accompanied St Nicholas on his rounds, ready to punish naughty children. But the Krampus stretched the evil helper figure further than all these other characters. Whereas Knecht Ruprecht was essentially a primal human and even the Czech 'Devils' were usually a man covered in soot, the Krampus was a demonic hell-beast resembling a horrifically mutated goat. Whilst Zwarte Piet might beat children with a birch rod, the Krampus had a sadistically wide range of punishments and tortures. True, he did use the birch rod on occasions, but he had in addition a whole repertoire of penalties that ranged from ripping out a girl's pigtails to leading children off cliffs Pied Piper-style or tossing children onto a train that was on a one-way journey to a lake of fire. He especially enjoyed eating naughty children for Christmas dinner, and he'd even carry a bathtub on his back just in case the mood took him to drown a child in a bathful of water – or sometimes ink – before fishing them out with his pitchfork to eat.

Krampus celebrations were often far more ambitious than the visits of Zwarte Piet and the other helpers. The Krampus would accompany St Nicholas on his private rounds, but he also made public appearances in his own right. For 5 December was not only St Nicholas's Eve, it was also Krampusnacht, the night when the Krampus was free to roam the Alpine streets, heading from house to house to demand tribute from adults, often in the form of alcohol.

Most traditions of demons and monsters roaming the winter streets were mere myths. People took precautions to protect themselves from the evil beings in question but did not really expect to actually encounter any monsters. Krampusnacht, however, was a different matter. Hordes of Krampusse* really did descend into

* The plural of a Krampus.

towns and villages in an event called the Krampuslaufen or the Running of the Krampus. The Krampusse in question were of course not really monsters; they were large groups of young local men dressed up in self-made costumes of fur, masks and goats' horns, charging around the streets with birch rods and pitchforks getting increasingly drunk, accusing people they encountered of misbehaviour and threatening to beat them up as punishment. Genuine monsters from the fires of Hell would probably have caused less destruction.

This 'evidence' that the Krampus existed meant children in Austria feared the monster long after their counterparts in the rest of Europe might have grown out of belief in imaginary beasts.

Whilst many of these other Christmas characters peaked during the fifteenth and sixteenth centuries, interest in and enthusiasm for the Krampus seems to have grown over time. The nineteenth-century invention of Christmas cards saw a huge increase in the number of Christmas images of the Krampus sent around the world. The images were generally intended to be comical, and something about the mischievousness and malevolence of the character clearly appealed, for Krampus cards were extremely popular. One card shows him holding a child in the air by his ears, with one hand tugging at each ear to pull them off. In other cards he is tugging a group of children off the edge of a cliff, beating children or driving off in a cart with a child in a sack on his back. Yet another card shows a group of children opening a box wrapped with shiny Christmas paper, only to find the Krampus hiding inside waiting for them. In a more modern twist he's piloting a biplane, scanning the ground for children to punish.

Occasionally the tables get turned. One card shows that a

small girl has managed to seize the Krampus's birch rod and it is the Krampus himself who is cowering in fear of her. In others children have banded together to take revenge on the Krampus by forcing *him* over the cliff and preserving themselves. Generally though, it is the Krampus who is doling out punishments.

Some of the cards have a clear sexual twist. The Krampus is sometimes seen romancing attractive ladies, and a couple of cards even show gigantic female Krampusse – far more woman than Krampus – chasing after adult men or carrying them away in her sack. This sexual theme for the Krampus would expand hugely after the sexual liberation of the 1960s, when cards often showed the fierce demonic figure invading the bedrooms of scantily clad women to beat them with his birch rod.

There's something about a wild, primal half-human half-beast with a passion for alcohol, sex and violence that has led to the Krampusse being unpopular with both the Church and governments. The Church has tried to ban him several times, and he has been the subject of numerous government interventions. There is even a story that Hitler attempted to ban the Krampus in Austria in the 1930s.

Unfortunately, appealing though the idea of the Krampus as a figure of anti-Nazi resistance might be, this is not quite true. The Krampus was indeed banned by a Fascist government in Austria, but this took place in 1934, four years before the Nazi Anschluss. In actual fact, the Nazis were fond of pagan imagery and German mythology, and preferred traditional Germanic characters like Knecht Ruprecht to Catholic figures like St Nicholas or Americans like Santa Claus. The Austro-fascist regime prior to the Nazis, however, was predominantly made up of ultra-conservative Catholics, and the fact that the Krampus had largely supplanted St Nicholas by this time and was delivering presents by himself did not go down well!

Opposition to the Krampus remained after the Second World War. In 1953 the head of Austria's kindergarten system, Dr Ernst Kotbauer, claimed that the fear of the Krampus could potentially psychologically damage children for life. Kotbauer felt there was too much fear in the world – he cited unemployment, high taxes and the atom bomb (all traditional children's concerns!) as examples – and that Austrians could start to make it a better place by doing without the Krampus. Unfortunately, he did not explain how banning a mythical Christmas figure would achieve full employment, lower taxes or nuclear disarmament but, if he can deliver on his promises, he'll certainly get my vote!

Dr Kotbauer entitled his leaflet 'The Krampus is an Evil Man', which is something I think both the creatures' fans and detractors would have agreed with. The question really came down to how much people enjoyed the evil. It seemed that the answer was 'too much to want to get rid of him', and the Krampus celebrations continued unabated. If anything the Krampus has subsequently grown in popularity.

Krampus festivities remain today, not only in Austria, but in parts of Germany, Croatia and Hungary. Local residents will line the streets to watch a traditional Krampuslaufen where, just as in medieval times, young men dressed as Krampusse charge through the streets. The tradition is to make your own costume, and these can be extremely elaborate with wooden masks and glowing red eyes powered by batteries. The Krampusse roam through the streets making ferocious animal sounds, charging at young children and attacking all who stand in their way with a birch rod. These days the attack is more symbolic than violent –

the bystander gets no more than a fright and a gentle tap with a rod – but the debate over its impact on children remains. In 2006 child psychologist Max Friedrich made yet another call for a ban, echoing Dr Kotbauer by arguing that the world was already an aggressive place and that the Krampus merely added to the levels of violence.[9]

A genuine problem with the celebration is that the Krampuslaufen retains, at its core, groups of young men getting drunk together and charging around the streets interfering with strangers. It is not unknown for things to get out of hand. This is nowhere near as much of a problem as in olden times, though. Young men playing the Krampusse in days gone by organised the processions themselves on an ad-hoc basis. Anecdotes suggest that they would frequently abandon their pursuit of naughty children and start charging after young women instead. Nonetheless, organisers of many contemporary Krampuslaufen insist on the masked devils each wearing a number, just so that the atmosphere and the anonymity don't lead to anything too regrettable.

That said, things do not always go wrong in quite the direction you would expect. In his essay 'Christmas Markets in the Tyrolean Alps[10]', Oliver Haid recounts an incident from a Christmas market in 2001 in which three Krampusse and one St Nicholas were hired to scare local children, but were a little bit shy and nervous. Children and teenagers cottoned on to the fear and began to chase them instead. The quartet ended up having to take refuge in a local pub for an hour as a gang of fifty youngsters surrounded the pub and pestered them to come out. What is the world coming to when even a Krampus is afraid to walk the streets at night?

4

Be Good for Goodness' Sake

Joulupukki (Finland)

Krampuslaufen aside, most of the characters we have talked about so far tended to arrive in the company of St Nicholas. No matter how scary Black Peter, the Devil or Père Fouettard were, children knew that the good Christian bishop St Nicholas was there to protect them. Nonetheless, eventually the likes of Belsnickel and the Krampus began to usurp Nicholas and carry out visits on their own.

They were not the only Christmas monster who was happy to pay individual visits. And they were far from alone in the realms of demonic figures that stalked the countryside around the Christmas period. Many European countries have traditional monsters for winter nights that seem to predate Christian influence.

The Kallikantzoroi

In Greece those twelve days of Christmas are also the time of the Kallikantzoroi – malevolent goblins who take different forms in different parts of the country. In some places they look like small humans, normally male, with prominent sexual organs. In other places they are huge scaly humanoid creatures as large as a building, with razor-sharp claws and no genitalia at all. They could even be half-human, half-beast, with gigantic heads, bright-red eyes and limbs like monkeys. However they appeared, the consistent thing was that they would wander rural Greece for twelve days at the darkest part of every winter.

The Kallikantzoroi spent the rest of the year underground, and their emergence was not entirely bad news – it actually saved the world! Greek tradition went that there was a tree of life that ran right through the Earth and acted as a scaffold to hold it in place. Without the tree, the Earth would simply collapse in on itself. The Kallikantzoroi are quite keen on world destruction and spend January to December sawing through the tree, hoping to snap it in half and bring down the Earth. By the end of the year only the slenderest of threads holds the tree together, and the world is set to end at any second. But, just as the Kallikantzoroi are about to make the final cut, Christmas arrives and they are summoned above ground. By the time they return in early January, the tree has regrown and they have to start all over again.

Perhaps this is the reason why the Kallikantzoroi tend to be quite angry about their enforced nocturnal roaming and take their anger out on the local population. Sometimes their actions are mischievous – they play pranks, steal things or sow discord amongst communities. Sometimes they take the slightly less subtle approach of sneaking down the chimney – where have we heard about that before? Once inside the house, they might simply overturn furniture and destroy possessions or they might move on to the inhabitants – beating people savagely or even aping Perchta and ripping out intestines.

The Kallikantzoroi have another trick up their sleeves – they like to steal newborn babies. On the upside, they do not – unlike the Krampus – actually eat the infants. The bad news is they instead turn them into fellow Kallikantzoroi. Parents knew that any baby born over the twelve days of Christmas might be spirited away during the night and be fated to spend eternity as one of these strange, sinister creatures (or at least turn into one for twelve nights each year). It is possible that this fate was intended as a punishment to discourage women from giving birth during the Christmas season. This may have been because it was considered a sin to draw attention away from Christ's birth.[11] However, it is also possible that the increased hazards of mid-winter births made it more desirable to encourage women to have spring or summer babies.

Still, there were precautions that could be taken to protect babies (and indeed whole households) from the Kallikantzoroi. Binding newborns with tresses of straw and garlic would ensure the creatures could not get near them. But how did you stop a Kallikantzoroi from getting near your house in the first place?

The answer was to confuse them. The Kallikantzoroi might have been fierce, mischievous and deadly, but they were not especially bright. That's just as well really – otherwise they might have had the willpower to resist the lure of the outside world at Christmas and instead complete their mission to destroy the Earth. One thing the Kallikantzoroi could not do was to count beyond two. This was not just a lack of numeracy skills – the number three was seen as a holy number by the Greeks. The creatures would count 'one, two' and get confused, lose count and have to start again. This meant that the Kallikantzoroi were easy to trick by simply placing a colander outside the front door. The creatures would feel compelled to count the holes and, of course, would not be able to do so. Their confusion and failure to count would keep them occupied until sunrise – at which point the household would be safe until darkness fell again. Other ruses might involve burning something with a strong smell or leaving meat in the chimney as a peace offering.

The origins of the Kallikantzoroi are not entirely clear, but one theory is that they are actually a form of werewolf. In

Germany and Poland there are traditions that werewolves roam every night for the twelve days of Christmas, and the idea of babies becoming Kallikantzoroi might simply be another version of this myth.

Karakoncolos

It is also possible that the Kallikantzoroi are related to the Karakoncolos, a Christmas creature from eastern Europe. This character appears in Bulgaria, Turkey, and Serbia and takes slightly different forms in each country, but generally resembles a cross between the Devil and a sasquatch. In Turkey, his behaviour often involves standing on street corners on winter nights waiting for passers-by and asking them riddles. If the traveller gives an answer that includes the word 'black', then the Karakoncolos lets them go on their way. But if the passer-by fails to use that word, or indeed fails to answer at all, the Karakoncolos strikes them dead with a single blow. Sometimes his behaviour is more that of a trickster who takes the form of a woman or young girl and appears at people's doors to con his way inside in order to be given food. Once inside the Karakoncolos feels compelled to imitate his host's behaviour. One way of getting rid of him is to set fire to some silk or thread. The Karakancolos will respond in kind by setting his own fur on fire and, upon realising what he has done, will run from the house screaming for water.

Sometimes the Karakoncolos turns up at people's houses for more sinister reasons. They sometimes use their powers of disguise to pretend to be a loved one and lure the householder out into the snow. Once outside, the person finds themselves caught in a trance and unable to move. They stand there frozen to the spot until the cold takes over and they wind up freezing to death.

Another favourite trick of the creature in parts of Serbia is to sneak into houses and linger behind the doorways of children's bedrooms. As the child goes through the doorway the Karakoncolos stretches out a hand and grabs the child by the neck before dragging them off to eat.

The Karakoncolos did not always kill its victims, however – particularly in Serbia it is known to use humans as its own personal taxi service. They again lure victims outside before placing them under a spell and leaping onto their back and forcing their captive to ferry them wherever they want to go. The exhausted victim is only released at dawn.

The Wild Hunt

Some of the richest midwinter folklore is that which comes from the Norse mythology of Scandinavia. The Normans were descended from the Vikings and inherited some of their mythology. As they took control of much of Europe over the Middle Ages, they managed to disseminate those myths, and the legends of their hero St Nicholas, across the European population. If many Christmas traditions descended from pagan origins, then the Norse and their Norman descendants were often the standard bearers of those traditions and, as such, were hugely influential.

Like the Germanic peoples of central Europe, many of the Norse traditions were based around the idea of the Wild Hunt; a tradition found right across northern and central Europe and believed to have been a key part of pre-Christian midwinter celebrations. The Wild Hunt was a ritual tied to the marking of the winter solstice and the rebirth of life for the coming year, and involved a great hunting party which swept through the midwinter skies some time between Yule and what would now be called Twelfth Night.

The leader of the hunt was usually said to be Odin (or his equivalent Woden in Germanic traditions). Odin was said to wear a red cloak and to ride an eight-legged horse called Sleipnir, throwing sweets and treats down to children as he went. Many researchers into paganism regard this as the 'true' origin of Santa Claus.

The make-up and purpose of the hunt both varied from country to country, but it was usually made up of the spirits of the dead searching for a final resting place. It was believed at the time that the souls of the dead would be carried away on the winds of the storm after their passing, and it was not until the next winter that Odin would be able to ride through the sky and channel those winds, leading the souls to a new home.

Alternative traditions, especially amongst Celtic and Gaelic communities, associated the hunt with faeries or what the Orkney and Shetland islanders called trows – small humanoid creatures that were thought to live unseen amongst humans, with their own customs and traditions. Whereas nowadays we think of fairies – the common modern spelling – as gentle, magical creatures who make wishes come true, the faeries of Gaelic folklore could be cruel and capricious. Tales exist of them stealing cattle, destroying crops or farmhouses and luring people to their lairs to spend the night. The unwise visitor would leave the following morning to find a whole year, or perhaps even whole generations, had passed.

As with the Kallikantzoroi, there were also traditions of faeries stealing babies. It was said they would approach houses during the night, spirit well-behaved infants away and replace them with a faerie lookalike. The only clue that this had happened was that the baby would change overnight from being placid and mild to being irritable, screaming and showing an almost demonic desire to frustrate the parents as much as possible. I'm sure many new parents will understand exactly how this myth began!

Faeries – and trows in particular – could be very violent too. Often they were said to hate Christianity, and stories exist of them killing priests who tried to rid neighbourhoods of their presence. Interestingly, some traditions suggest that faeries and trows may actually be the restless souls of the unbaptised dead, so their presence on the Wild Hunt might not actually be a significant deviation from the Norse tradition. Certainly Yule, Hallowe'en and New Year's Eve were key times of faerie and trow activity, and it may not be coincidence that these are also the nights when the dead are said to be most active.[12]

Whether it was made up of the undead, faeries or both, the other key feature of the Wild Hunt was the significance of dogs, which tended to accompany the hunt in large numbers. Dogs played a key role in some pagan mythologies as people held the belief that a person's soul could not be set free until the flesh had left the bones. The ghostly dogs that accompanied the hunt, therefore, were often thought to be there to consume the flesh of the restless dead and, in doing so, help them to find a peaceful home.[13] There were also stories of people whose houses had been passed by the Wild Hunt finding a small black puppy in their fireplace. If they did not look after this puppy, very bad luck would come to them over the next year.

If this was a Wild Hunt, what were they hunting for? Again, the quarry of the Wild Hunt varied significantly from place to place. Sometimes it was the elusive resting place of the dead, sometimes it was a mythical wild boar and sometimes it was fairy maidens. Other traditions say the Hunt was searching for lost travellers, liars or men or women who had dishonoured themselves.

In fact, it was perhaps dishonoured women – especially prostitutes, witches and priests' concubines – that featured most of all. Such people were said to be captured and killed by the hunting party and then, for all eternity, would be forced to join their number. In some folk stories – particularly in Gaelic traditions – the 'loose' woman would be transformed into a hare and any priests who had sinned with her into hunting dogs, damned to chase after her for eternity. Other stories told of the hunt often comprising children who had died without being baptised and who were thus denied entry to Heaven. Sometimes these children would be the prey of the hunt, whilst sometimes they became the hunting dogs pursuing their neglectful parents.

In western Norway the Wild Hunters were known as Julereia (or Yule Riders) or Oskoreia (from a word meaning 'terror'). As in other traditions, the hunt consisted of the dead, but here it was people who been judged neither good enough for Heaven nor evil enough for Hell and so were doomed to ride the night skies for evermore. They would cause chaos as they went over houses, smashing household items, replacing casks of ale with casks of water and spiriting away livestock, leaving only the hooves behind. They were not wholly bad, however – if you left out a gift such as beer or bread, then the farm would be unharmed and was said to meet with good luck the following year.

All across Europe, seeing the Wild Hunt, or even simply encountering one of its gigantic, fiery-eyed, black hellhounds was thought a terrible omen – especially if you tried to interact with the dead procession. Potential side effects of encountering the hunt included death, madness or being swept away and killed by an army of dead vigilantes. Even if you avoided death or destruction yourself, it might mean your country was doomed to face a terrible war or a national tragedy.

Nonetheless, stories exist of people who did survive encounters with Wild Hunts. Orderic of Vitalis, a cleric in Normandy, told of a priest called Walchelin who encountered a vast army on New Year's Day 1091 and recognised among the warriors people whom he knew to have recently died. All of them were being punished for sins committed during their lifetime. Greedy and selfish men were chained down by the weight of their possessions. A murderer was strapped to a beam and was being violated by a demon. Loose, sinful women were tormented with hot burning nails penetrating their buttocks and thighs as punishment for their 'sensuous lechery'.[14] Horses and mules carried the wandering army, and Walchelin spotted empty carriages pulled by the horses of women who were still alive. Interestingly, there were also a great number of priests and bishops who had clearly sinned in ways that Walchelin was not aware of.

Walchelin then encountered a group of dead knights on enormous horses, still clad in battle armour and ready for war. Just like the sinful women, they were accompanied by horses that were yet to find a rider. Realising he was witnessing the Wild Hunt, Walchelin decided to obtain proof of his encounter by stealing one of the unmanned horses. This did not go well. As soon as his foot touched the stirrup he received a tremendous burn, and as soon he touched the saddle he felt a terrible chill.

Worse still, he immediately found himself surrounded by angry knights threatening to drag him off with the hunt, never to return. The good news was that he was then rescued by another knight, who agreed to grant Walchelin his life, if he would only pass a message on to the dead knight's wife. The bad news was that Walchelin realised that if he started passing on messages from the dead, he would be dismissed as both a fool and a sinner and lose his job, reputation and place in Heaven. Personally, I think he might have messed that last one up when he decided to steal a demonic hell-horse!

In any case, Walchelin refused the request, so the knight grabbed him around the neck and prepared to strike his fatal blow. Walchelin was only saved by the intercession of his recently deceased brother who, he was distraught to learn, was himself amongst the procession of dead sinners. His brother told Walchelin that he deserved to die for stealing the horse but would be granted his life as he had said Mass earlier that day. With that, Walchelin was released, but the scar from the knight's grip caused a permanent disfigurement.

There were other encounters with the Wild Hunt. Monks at Peterborough Abbey in 1127 reported seeing horrific-looking demonic hunters riding horses, goats and sheep, accompanied by black dogs with fiery eyes – although this was actually at Easter rather than Christmas. Earlier, in 1123 Abbot Ekkehard reported that the residents of Worms in Saxony encountered a multitude of ghostly armed horsemen. Some of the braver locals armed themselves with a cross and questioned the horse-men at length, and they confirmed they were the souls of recently departed knights.

In Norse mythology, people who assisted the hunt in good faith were rewarded with the gift of a horse's leg which, if kept until the next day, would change into a lump of gold. However, in Germany showing an interest in the hunt could have particularly gruesome consequences. There is a story of a peasant overhearing a Wild Hunt that was pursuing a woodwife (a female fairy spirit that lived in the wood and guarded animals from unwelcome huntsmen). The leader of the hunt made a hunting call and the peasant decided to return it. Perhaps he was encouraging the huntsman, perhaps he was mocking him, or perhaps he was just caught up in the moment – it is hard to say for sure – but, whatever his motive, he was rewarded the next day when he went out to his stable and found he had been given his share of the spoils – one quarter of a woodwife hanging from the stable door.

This is not an isolated story – other accounts tell of ordinary people showing an interest in the Wild Hunt and later being rewarded by a fetid human limb appearing down the chimney. If you think this German folklore is a little tasteless, the UK manages to top it. A farmer on Dartmoor saw the Wild Hunt one night and, trying to alleviate his fear with humour, he jokingly called out to one of the horsemen, requesting a share of the spoils of their hunt. To his surprise, the horsemen threw him a package which felt like the body of an animal wrapped in a bundle. The farmer carried it home with him. When he arrived, he laid the package on the table and eagerly unwrapped it. The 'meat' he found inside was the body of his own child.

The Origins of the Wild Hunt

As I have said, the Wild Hunt is usually linked to Norse traditions. Odin – or in Germany Woden – is said to be the original Wild Huntsman and it is believed to be a tradition that had been prevalent for centuries prior to the coming of Christianity. This commonly held belief about the Wild Hunt is singularly hard to establish for certain.

One of the main reasons for this is that most people who wrote about and recorded the Wild Hunts were connected to the Church and Christianity. This is not particularly surprising in itself – literacy levels were exceptionally low and only the clergy and the wealthy elite tended to be able to read and write. There was even a law in twelfth-century England that stated that if you could read and recite a passage from the Bible you were legally considered a member of the clergy. This was hugely important for well-educated – and therefore almost certainly rich – laymen, as being a member of the clergy entitled you to shorter sentences for whatever crimes you committed.

Unfortunately, this means that most of our information from the eleventh and twelfth centuries about medieval beliefs in the Wild Hunt comes from the point of view of people who regarded them as sinful, heathen practices and wanted to replace them with something more religiously appropriate. Consequently, accounts of the Wild Hunt depicting it as an unholy army of the unbaptised dead who tormented everyone they encountered might possibly be a little biased.

This makes the origins of the Wild Hunt extremely hard to trace. Certainly there are Norse traditions of Odin and the Valkyries riding through the sky and collecting those who have died in battle. It is easy to see how this could have been supplanted onto the tradition of the Wild Hunt, but much of our understanding of Norse mythology derives from the *Poetic Edda*, a collection of poems and verse that were first collected in the twelfth and thirteenth centuries. The poems themselves are oral folktales passed down by generations of minstrels and are undoubtedly older than that, but exactly when and where they originate – and how exactly they relate to the development of the myths – is not completely clear. Odin *could* have been the original Wild Huntsman, but whether he was or not is a different question. The evidence for Woden being the first hunt leader in Germany is sketchy at best[15] and, even in areas like south

Sweden and Jutland where Odin is definitely identified as the leader of the Wild Hunt, it's unclear whether this identification is supported by evidence in ancient traditions or is based on a more recent reinterpretation of the Wild Hunt which tries to tie it to other myths about the Norse Gods.[16]

An equally pertinent question is whether the Wild Hunt was actually a pre-Christian ritual at all – at least in the form in which Christian writers describe it. These chroniclers may have observed or overheard pagan processions of men in animal costumes charging around the countryside, making lots of noise and engaging in non-Christian practices, and visualised them as monsters or armies of the dead and the doomed out to wander the Earth. It is possible that a young monk, fervent with religious belief and closeted from the outside world, attributed a very different meaning to a relatively innocent ceremony. In fact, even if the writer knew he was watching people in masks, he might have assumed them to be possessed by the undead or demons and forced to act in such a manner by the Devil and the forces of evil. And – even if they did not literally believe such possessions to have taken place – it's easy to see how Christian missionaries might have been tempted to interpret the events as evil so as to warn their flock of the dangers of participating in sinful heathen rituals.

This is an appealing theory – and quite amusing, as it would potentially lead to the brilliantly surreal situation where modern-day pagans who observe pre-Christian rituals are actually observing rituals invented by Christians in order to discourage medieval pagans from practising paganism – but it ignores the fact that both the idea of the dead and demons walking the Earth at Christmas and indeed traditions of Wild Hunts are spread far and wide across Europe. Plus, certain touches – the hunt riding through the sky on storms, for example – tally far more convincingly with Nordic or faerie traditions than they do with anything the Christians invented; it seems likely that the hunt does have pre-Christian roots, even if it is hard to say exactly what form it originally took or whether Odin was its original leader.

Lussinatta

The Norwegian Wild Hunt, meanwhile, was led by a female figure – that of Lussi. Nowadays Lussi is best remembered in Sweden and Norway as St Lucia and 13 December is St Lucia's Day. St Lucia is represented as a beautiful young woman and the day is marked by a procession. A local girl is selected to play the saint. She dresses in white with a red sash and wears a crown of candles on her head. She will parade through the town followed by a series of similarly white-clad girls, each clutching a candle and singing songs dedicated to the saint.

Although St Lucia (or St Lucy) is indeed a historical saint, this is actually a relatively recent celebration which began in Sweden in the eighteenth or nineteenth century. But Norway actually celebrated a Lucia (or Lussi) centuries earlier, albeit in a very different form. For the night before 13 December was the Lussinatta or Lucy Night. This was the night when evil spirits and demons rose up to wander the Earth, which they then continued to do every night until Yule arrived a week or so later. This of course ties in with myths elsewhere in Europe. Hungarians also see Lucy Night as a night of demonic activity and witchcraft.

In these wanderings, Lussi was a hideously evil she-demon with magical powers. She was said to ride through the skies on a broomstick accompanied by demons, evil spirits and trolls, spreading mayhem and chaos wherever she went. Like Perchta, she was keen to ensure Christmas celebrations had been prepared effectively and, like Zwarte Piet or the Krampus, she wanted to make sure children had behaved throughout the year. The children needed to be good and the adults needed to ward off evil by protecting their homes with the sign of the cross. Otherwise Lussi would make her move – destroying property, crops or livestock, and kidnapping or killing badly behaved children.

This led to a tradition called Lussevaka, where households would stay awake all night the day before Lussinatta in order to guard their property and ensure evil spirits did not harm them or their families. Nowadays, this ritual is mostly kept alive by students hosting all-night parties to mark Lucy Night. Other preparations could also be made to ward off the spirits. In Norway it's customary to hide all the brooms in the house on Christmas Eve in order to ensure the witches and evil spirits don't steal them and join the Lussinatta procession.

Lussi, like so many of these characters, has gradually developed in parts of Europe from a demon to the bringer of gifts. In Böhmerwald, Austria, she has taken the role of the Krampus or Knecht Ruprecht, dressing as a she-goat and handing out fruits to good children whilst threatening to slit the bellies of those who misbehave. At the beginning of the twentieth century in Tyrol she would actually share gift-giving duties with St Nicholas – Nicholas giving to the boys and Lussi to the girls.

There is also a related tradition in the Shetlands – which for much of the Middle Ages had closer ties with Scandinavia than it did with mainland Scotland – of Tulya's Eve. Tulya's Eve came a week before Yule and was often seen as the beginning of the Yule period. It was the night where the trows – those mischievous goblins or faeries – were free to emerge from their lairs and wander the Earth causing mischief. Residents would attempt to protect livestock, crops and property with the sign of the cross – making crosses out of straw for the entrance to the farm and out of pleated cow or horse hair to cover the entrance to the stable. That and a blazing peat fire (which gives off a scent said to repel trows) were said to be enough to keep evil from your door and ensure your property was safe for the night.

Many parts of Scandinavia also had similar traditions of trolls coming out to make mischief. In Sweden, Christmas Eve was said to be the night of trolling. Another Scandinavian tradition had it that 24 December was the night that the dead returned to visit their descendants. Families would make very careful preparations to ensure the dead had a decent welcome. A fire would be maintained all night, a feast would be left on the table and sometimes even a hot bath was prepared. In some parts of Sweden, people would make their beds with clean sheets but then sleep on straw on the floor, leaving the bed free in case the trolls or the dead chose to use them.

Sweden had a particular tradition of a creature called a tomte, who was a (usually) benign fairy or troll. Each household – and particularly each farm – would have its own tomte and, as long as they were kept happy, they would look after the farm and guarantee its prosperity and luck. The tomte was both a traditionalist and a perfectionist and, like Lussi, would get very angry and upset if traditions and customs were not observed the 'right' way. At Christmas, it was important to please the tomte with a gift of porridge – left in a bowl overnight. Sometimes he was left clothes, drink or tobacco too. Failure to leave gifts could mean that the tomte would leave – taking all the farm's good luck with him and thus dooming the farm for the coming year – or turn malevolent and play tricks such as destroying things, tying animal's tails together or leaving doors and windows open during the freezing winter nights. The tomte could even turn violent and beat people for depriving him of his porridge.

Even when he did bring riches and prosperity, the tomte was not always a good thing for Swedish farms. Puritans and church reformers who were keen to phase out pagan traditions equated the tomte with the Devil and related it to wicked, sinful and unchristian practice. Unfortunately, this meant that successful farmers during particularly strict religious times risked opening themselves up to accusations that their farm was thriving due to the presence of a tomte – which was basically tantamount to being 'outed' as a witch during the Inquisitions of the Middle Ages and could be extremely dangerous for the farmer. Nowadays the tomte has had a startling rehabilitation – he's grown a beard, donned a red suit and started looking and acting remarkably like the American Santa Claus.

The Yule Goat

Another traditional Scandinavian figure was that of the Yule Goat. Known as Julebukk in Norway, Julsvenn in Sweden and Joulupukki in Finland he – like the tomte – has gradually mutated into a Santa figure but started off as something very, very different. Traditions change from place to place, but the general rule was that the Yule Goat was a caprine beast – possibly an invisible caprine beast – who arrived just before the pagan midwinter festivities to ensure that everything was being prepared on schedule and in the correct manner.

In Sweden and Norway today, the Yule Goat is represented by a small straw goat which is essentially a tree decoration. There is a game played in parts of Norway where people try to hide their Yule Goat in a neighbour's house. If the neighbour then finds it, they must then hide it in another house and so on around the village.

In 1966 a business association in the Swedish town of Gävle started a tradition of building a gigantic Yule Goat and displaying it in the town to promote tourism. Unfortunately for them, that same year some local residents started a tradition of setting fire to the gigantic Yule Goat at the earliest possible opportunity.

Now every year a cat-and-mouse game is played between the constructors and local youths, where the builders of the goat try technique after technique to keep it standing and local youths find ways to destroy it – Yule Goats now appear elsewhere in Sweden too and often meet similar fates. In Gävle the goat goes up at the beginning of December and usually it is burned down around Lucy's Night, Christmas Eve or New Year's Eve. In 1999 it was burned down within two hours of construction. It does not always get burned down though – it has also been run over, stolen and thrown in a river. Perhaps the best story is the year that security guards were hired to give the goat 24-hour protection. All went well until one freezing night when the guards nipped into a nearby restaurant to momentarily warm themselves with a shot of a spirit. They went in and ordered their drinks. No sooner had they walked to the window and raised their glasses to their lips when they glanced outside and saw that the goat was already ablaze . . .

The roots of the Yule Goat appear to go back not to Christmas – or even to Yule – but to a Harvest Festival which, in Finland at least, was called Kekri.[17] Kekri happened between September and November (depending on when the harvest was finished) and acted both as a ritual of thanks for the harvest and to guarantee a good one the following year. Kekri was said to be the protector of cattle and crops and was represented by the Kekripukki (or Kekri goat). A ceremony would take place where dead ancestors would be remembered and thanked, and then there would be a drunken party around a bonfire, the aim of which was to get the host as drunk as possible. The belief was that a drunken host was an omen for a great harvest the following year, and the way the host swayed on his feet would represent the healthy crops billowing in the field come next summer. However, it was very important that the host remained standing – for if he fell over in a drunken stupor, the crops would surely go the same way. On the second day of the festival there would be further drunken parties in people's houses. At some point in the evening proceedings would be interrupted by the arrival of a procession led by Kekripukki – played by a local bachelor who had turned his fur coat inside out and constructed himself a pair of horns. Other unmarried men (and sometimes women) would dress in animal costumes and accompany him. The Kekripukki would travel from home to home and request alcohol or food, which the hosts would give him. There was a seedier side to this too – he was also allowed to invite women to sit on his lap, a request the women were compelled to obey.

There was a second goat too – a creature called the Nuutpukki. The Nuutpukki is thought to have originated in Sweden and would visit houses on a second festival (presumably called Nuut) on 13 January, which was essentially a feast to finish off the Yule leftovers. On that night gangs of young men (and maybe women) in animal costumes would maraud through the town, demanding tributes from householders in the form of food or alcohol. Like the Krampuslaufen, the Nuutpukki procession could easily turn into a frightening, drunken pillage. A tradition also began to emerge of the Nuutpukki beating naughty children with birch rods or rewarding well-behaved children with sweets.

Like most pagan celebrations, the Yule Goat was not terribly popular with Christians. Finland was predominantly a Lutheran country and, after the Reformation, the Church attempted to dispense with this pesky pagan nonsense – anyone publicly celebrating Kekri or Nuut risked punishment. Midwinter celebrations shifted to focus on the end of December, and the traditions of the Kekripukki or the Nuutpukki first of all became the Joulupukki – the Yule or Christmas Goat – before the Church attempted to phase it out altogether. Stories began to circulate linking Joulupukki with the Devil, and tales 'proving' the goat was evil began to emerge.

There was a story where a girl danced at midnight with a straw Yule Goat, only to suddenly find that the goat had somehow changed form and she was literally dancing with the Devil. There was a man who dressed up as a traditional pagan Yule Goat and found himself immediately spirited away by an angry Beelzebub, furious that somebody had dared to impersonate him. In Finland, the Yule Goat became a terrifying figure who would appear just before the festive period, demanding gifts of tribute and punishing (and sometimes eating) naughty children.

Eventually the Yule Goat became this Christmas Goat and his behaviour softened. By the middle of the twentieth century he had gone from demander of tribute to seasonal gift-giver. The 1940s Swedish children's book *Peter and Lotta's Christmas* tells the story of two children staying with their uncle and aunt in the Swedish countryside and being understandably shocked when a bipedal talking goat turns up during their Christmas

Eve meal, asks them if they have been good and hands them some presents!*

By the end of the twentieth century the Christmas Goat had changed in appearance. Like the tomte, he turned into a man, grew a big white beard and acquired a natty red suit with a black belt. His name in Finland – Joulupukki – might still mean Yule Goat but in all other respects he is Santa Claus.

Finland is one of the few places in Europe today where Santa visits children whilst they are still awake, rather than sneaking in unannounced during the night. Sometimes this might be a family member or a friend in disguise, but there are also companies that you can hire to take your presents from you and send a Joulu-pukki to deliver – often this is work that will be undertaken by students or young people looking for casual work. My friend Juha – who is Finnish himself and has helped me out with lots of my research – played Joulupukki once. He tells me that part of the custom is that every house will offer Santa a spirit – which decorum and manners dictate that he must accept. This is not too much of a problem earlier in the evening, but households at the end of 'Santa's' list will end up being called on by a drunken student who can barely speak or stand upright!

Despite this, in Europe at least, Joulupukki is possibly the most successful Christmas gift-giver of all, for it has become accepted across the rest of Europe that Finnish Lapland – where he is said to have his home – is in fact the home of Santa Claus for all Europeans.

Finnish Lapland is also the setting for the 2010 cult Finnish film *Rare Exports*, which focuses on a young boy growing up at the foot of the Korvatunturi mountain, which is seen in Finland

* Their uncle is mysteriously absent from the room during the goat's visit!

as the 'official home' of Father Christmas. He discovers that Santa Claus exists, but far from being the figure children know and love today, the real Santa Claus is a gigantic caprine demon who, in ancient times, roamed Lapland kidnapping and killing naughty children.

The film is imaginative, clever and a lot of fun and, as director Jalmari Helander explains, deeply rooted in local mythology: 'The evil Santa comes from the mythology of this folklore. We actually have this very scary Santa character. And the idea was originally from ... I saw some pictures of this evil Santa with horns. There are a lot of interesting stories in many European countries about Santa Claus. The original legends are quite scary, it's interesting'[18]

The Staalo

Despite the creature's resemblance to the Yule Goat, it may not actually be Joulupukki that Helander is talking about. The people of Lapland – the Sami – are historically a separate people from the Finns, Swedes and Norwegians, and they had their own set of traditions. And what traditions they were! For they had a Yule figure of their own – the Joulustaalo. Many of the characters in this book are disturbing, but nobody – not the Krampus, not Joulupukki and not even the Yule Lads who I'll discuss in the next chapter – can compete with a Joulustaalo for sheer unremitting psychotic destructive bastardry.

Stories about exactly *what* the Staalo was varied according to time and place, but essentially he was a huge, mean creature who lived alone in the wilderness of the snows of Lapland. Sometimes he was simply a very large Neanderthal man, sometimes an evil wizard and sometimes half-troll or half-devil.

Some people believed the Staalo to be one creature, whereas others claim the Staalos were actually an entire race, albeit one that was so aggressive that they avoided each other and so were never seen together. But one thing everyone agreed on was that there was nothing they enjoyed more than causing pain, and no meal they enjoyed more than human flesh. Ideally children's flesh.

Often the Staalo was accompanied by a huge, fierce hunting dog on sorties to find children to steal, cook and eat. He also brandished a large silver knife and would turn up at an isolated house or hut in Lapland, demand to speak to the master of the house and challenge him to a knife fight or a wrestling match. If the Staalo won then everyone inside the hut was his to kill and eat. If the human won then the Staalo would offer the unsuspecting human his knife and invite the victor to kill him with it. Unfortunately, the knife had magic properties that would actually heal the Staalo and allow him to gain strength and kill his antagonist as revenge. Only people who had the sense to use their own knife could successfully kill the Staalo. They would be rewarded with all the Staalo's gold and possessions.

Initially the Staalo was not actually a Christmas creature but more of an all-purpose bad guy for Sami folktales. Though incredibly strong, Staalos were not very bright, and many Lap folktales told of cunning heroes who managed to outsmart the creature and escape with their lives. Anyone who managed to kill a Staalo was seen as a hero in Sami culture.

Christianity was first introduced to the Sami in the thirteenth century and had been adopted by most Sami by the eighteenth century. Christmas Eve was seen as the holiest day of the year and was the day when the preparations had to take place for the entire Christmas season. For example, enough water had to be carried into the *kota* (the name of the tepee-like tents in which most Sami people lived) and enough wood had to be chopped so that the family had supplies for the entire Christmas season. Cleaning and tidying was important too – the area around the *kota* should be cleared of obstructions such as branches, skis or sledges, and the ground needed to be swept and tidied.

As in other parts of Scandinavia, the Samis believed that Christmas Eve was also the night when invisible, evil creatures were able to roam the Earth. At some point – and it is not entirely clear when or how – the Staalo became involved with Christmas traditions and a version of him emerged called the Joulustaalo (or Christmas Staalo). The Joulustaalo would spend the night transporting hay for Christmas and would ride around on a sledge pulled by one of each of the animals of the forest – shrews, mice, lemmings, foxes, wolves, bears and so forth – with the smallest creature at the front and the bear at the back. The Joulustaalo did not like to be interrupted or hindered in his journey.

If his route was blocked by objects on the ground outside a tent that had not been tidied up properly, he would leap up from his sled, storm inside and murder anyone in the *kota*.

If his animals were disturbed by the sounds of children talking inside the tent, he would leap up from his sled, storm inside and murder anyone in the *kota*.

If there was not sufficient water inside a tent, he would leap up from his sled, storm inside and . . . you can guess the rest.

Water was extremely important as, if confronted by the Joulustaalo, it could be the difference between life and death. There was a story of a boy called Uula Sammeli who had

101

forgotten to clean up outside his *kota* and, as a result, the Joulustaalo's sled got caught in some branches of the trees. Uula Sammeli rushed outside to clear them up, whilst the Joulustaalo threatened him and the animals screamed in frustration. It was only by giving the Joulustaalo some water that the boy managed to save himself.

If the Joulustaalo could not find any water, he would drink his favourite substitute – the blood and brains of a child. He would burst into the tent clutching an iron pipe, which he would first employ as a weapon to bash the child's skull in and then use as a straw to suck up the gooey treat inside.

Children had to be very careful around Christmas, and especially Christmas Eve, to ensure they kept themselves safe from the Joulustaalo. For example, children had to eschew going out alone on Christmas Eve, certainly had to avoid sledging down hills after dark (for who knew if the Joulustaalo was lurking at the bottom?), and it was absolutely essential that they avoided making any sounds after dark for, if the Joulustaalo heard them, he was sure to devour them.

The most vicious demonstration of the Joulustaalo's appetites comes from a story told by Sami wolf hunter Johan Turi, the first person to ever publish a non-religious work in the Sami language. Writing at the beginning of the twentieth century, Turi told a story from his own childhood. It is a tragic and horrible tale of children's games getting terribly out of hand and was used to terrify Lapp children into good behaviour. Be warned – of all the stories featured in this book this is almost certainly the most horrific and is not for the faint-hearted.

One Christmas there were a rich family and a poor family living in tents at the bottom of the Durkehanvarre mountain in Norway. The rich parents left their children – of which they had several – at home whilst they went to church.

The children decided to play a game of killing and gutting a reindeer – something their father would often do as reindeer were so essential to survival in Lapland. There were no reindeer available, so one of the children agreed to play the part of the reindeer and be bound for the slaughter. At this point things went nightmarishly wrong. The children were young and did not really understand the consequences of their actions and, in the course of playing at killing and gutting their brother, the oldest took a knife and did exactly what they had seen their father do. He slit his brother open from top to toe, pulled out all of his intestines and – as would be the next logical step in the process – began to cook his flesh.

So far, so utterly horrifying. But at this point, things got even worse. The scent of roasting human flesh was so appealing that Joulustaalo appeared on the scene and decided to treat himself to a meal. Of course, one child was not enough to satiate a hungry Joulustaalo. He wanted all of them. The younger ones fled and hid, but Joulustaalo captured the older ones and began to cook them. The younger children could do nothing but lie in their hiding places and watch without saying a word. Unfortunately, when Joulustaalo crunched the heads of the older children between his teeth, the younger children overheard the sound and cried out in shock. Joulustaalo heard their voices and knew where they were hiding. So he strolled to their hiding place, plucked them out one by one and threw them into the cooking pot. He then proceeded to devour them too.

Fortunately, the youngest child was hidden away from

the other children. She hid herself in a chest and managed to lock it from the inside so that Joulustaalo could not get to her. Joulustaalo knew where she was and did everything he could to reach her but he could not open the trunk. If this were a folktale from elsewhere in Europe – one told by Grimm, for example – the cunning child would have kept herself safe, outsmarted the Joulustaalo and found a way to bring her siblings back from the grave.

This is not a Grimm folktale.

Instead, frustrated by being unable to reach her, the Joulustaalo went to the fire and took some burning embers. He blew the embers through the keyhole of the trunk and kept doing this until the youngest girl died too, so now all the children had been slaughtered. As I said before, the Joulustaalo truly was an evil bastard.

Of course, the story does not end there. Whilst Joulustaalo had managed to kill everyone in the rich tent – and presumably leave behind a horrific scene for when the parents later returned from church – there was still the question of what happened in the poor tent next door.

In the poor tent there was an old woman, a young child and a dog. When the old woman heard the Joulustaalo arrive she hushed the child and dog and bound their mouths so they could not make a sound. This sounds harsh but it saved both of their lives for – and herein lies both the moral of the story and almost certainly the reason why parents were so fond of telling it to their children – if you did not make a sound on Christmas Eve, the Joulustaalo could not hurt you.

Nonetheless, the Joulustaalo had not yet quite finished his reign of destruction. Not long after he had finished his Christmas Eve meal, a girl turned up driving a herd of reindeer. She was wearing three coats, one on top of the other, to protect her from the cold. Joulustaalo pursued her too – for he wanted a further meal. Three times he tried to grab her, but each time he did so she slipped off one of her coats just in the nick of time, and he found himself holding a coat but no girl. The good news was that folklore and tradition said that the Joulustaalo was not allowed to try and grab someone a fourth time. The bad news was that Joulustaalo was allowed to summon up his demonic hunting dog and send it after the girl. The good news is the girl had a sack of bones which she used to delay the hound by throwing one each time he got close. The bad news is she never quite managed to lose him.

Eventually though, she and her reindeer herd did get home to the safety of her parents. She ran inside the tent and told them what had happened. Unfortunately, there were two problems. Firstly, the parents did not actually believe her story. Secondly, she was so exhausted from her trauma that she simply collapsed and died on the spot. And her reindeer died too.

Regrettably, the parents still did not believe the story and – call it stoicism, pragmatism or an incredibly curious reaction to grief – their first response to the situation was to cook the reindeer meat. Unfortunately, as they did so, the reindeer turned to stone.

This was undoubtedly a strange turn of events, but still the parents did not believe the Joulustaalo or anything supernatural could be involved, so they did not find a priest or somebody who could help rid them of the evil monster. Instead they simply went back to their tent – where the Joulustaalo was already waiting for them.

The next part of the story possibly sums up the wonderfully unhinged world of the Joulustaalo. For the Joulustaalo approached the parents and did three things. First of all, he cut off the man's penis and testicles. Secondly, he cut off the woman's breasts. Thirdly, he berated them for their poor parenting.

Lecture over, he turned both them and the remaining reindeer herd to stone and went on his way.

I've said it before and I'll say it again. There is nothing more evil than Joulustaalo.

Evil Goblins and Child-Eating Cats

The Yule Lads (Iceland)

When I say, 'There is nothing more evil than Joulustaalo,' I should actually say, 'There is nothing more evil than Joulustaalo outside of Iceland.'

Grýla and Leppalúði

Icelandic children are told of two trolls named Grýla and Leppalúði, whose existence in folklore and mythology dates back to at least the thirteenth century and who are said to be the most vicious and evil trolls in all the world. The male troll, Leppalúði, is bedridden and thus relatively powerless but the female troll, Grýla, is said to spend her time out searching for unruly children to kidnap and take home and boil in a pot for her and her husband to eat. She is often characterised as an ugly, vicious ogress with hooves and up to fifteen tails, plus excellent hearing that enables her to detect the slightest of childhood misdemeanours. Grýla's hearing is so acute that children know that, even if they manage to hide their wrongdoings from their parents, she will surely track them down and bundle them into a sack to take home as a meal.

This combination of omnipresence and lethal violence made Grýla a source of real horror to children, and from the fourteenth century onwards she was used as a bogeyman by parents to terrify their errant offspring into good behaviour. Whilst Grýla had similarities with Perchta in Italy and Germany, there was initially no evidence of an association of the ogress with

Christmas in Iceland, save of course for the fact that the forbidding atmosphere of the dark winter nights meant stories of a terrifying child-eating creature of the shadows had a particularly strong resonance in December, and hence was an incredibly effective deterrent to naughty children around this time of year.

Sometime around 1600, however, that began to change and Grýla began to be linked to a new mythology – that of the Yule Lads, one of the most bizarre and brilliant creations in all European Christmas mythology.

The Yule Lads

If we accept that many of the characters in this book serve as a metaphor for surviving the tough conditions of winter, it is perhaps not too surprising that Iceland produces some of the best stories of all. It is the most isolated and sparsely populated country in Europe and traditionally had an economy based on agriculture and fishing, despite only one fifth of its land being suitable for farming. It had no Industrial Revolution until 1900 and was one of the poorest and least-developed countries in the world. Furthermore, there are only four or five hours of daylight during December. Aside from the weather, its culture is shaped by years of oppressive Danish rule, several long drawn-out wars of independence and a frequent threat from active volcanoes – the worst of which, in 1783, killed half of the country's livestock, created a famine and released gases that ultimately killed one quarter of all Icelanders. In Icelandic mythology the consequences of isolation, domination by outside forces, torment by adverse weather conditions, long winter nights, mysterious deaths by poisoned air and strange lights in the sky all combine to create some of the most strange, imaginative and vicious mythology in the world. And the Yule Lads are perhaps the perfect example of this.

The Yule Lads are ogres that visit houses in the thirteen days before Christmas and stay until Twelfth Night. Although in some versions of the mythology there are several hundred different Yule Lads, the generally accepted modern belief is that they are thirteen in number, with one arriving each night from 12 December onwards and one leaving each night from 25 December onwards, thus meaning the final Yule Lad departs the house on 6 January.

Sometimes the Yule Lads were mere pranksters who playfully performed tricks and mischief to frustrate the inhabitants of each home, but many early accounts of their visits depict them as fearsome, remorseless monsters. Gratuitous violence, brutal murder and virtually every torture imaginable were associated with them, as they spirited misbehaving children away and devoured them in the bloodiest manner possible. It seems likely that in some regions telling stories of the Yule Lads became a competitive activity, as each teller tried to reach a level of cruelty and horror that surpassed all the others and took the story to new heights.

With such a predilection for violence it is perhaps not surprising that the Yule Lads came to be associated with Grýla and Leppalúði, and before long the story went that the Yule Lads were in fact children of these monstrous ogres, who had raised them to continue and, if possible, expand upon their evil bidding. Sometimes they'd merely mutilate a child, sometimes they'd kill them on the spot and other times they'd seize them and take them back to the family cave to cook and devour.

However, they were not merely creatures of violence – each

Yule Lad has his own unique characteristic and goal, and the purpose of the visit would not be merely child brutality but also a need to satiate other, more curious, urges.

In the traditional version now accepted as canonical, the first visitor was Sheep-Cote Clod, who was a Yule Lad with an ambition to harass the local sheep and suckle the ewes' milk. He was thwarted in his attempts to do so by his legs being as stiff as a board, so he could not bend down.

On 13 December Gully Gawk would arrive and await his opportunity to sneak into the cowshed and slurp up all the froth from the milk in the milking buckets.

Next came Stubby, the third and shortest of the Yule Lads. He would hang around the kitchen waiting for a chance to steal the frying pan from the stove and gobble up any bits of food that had stuck to the bottom of the pan.

The fourth visitor was Spoon Licker. As the name suggests, he liked to steal wooden spoons, with the intention of licking off any food residue.

On 16 December the Yule Lad to arrive was the equally literally named Pot Scraper, who liked to smuggle away pots that had not yet been washed and lick the contents.

The theme of petty culinary-related larceny continues on the 17th when Bowl Licker arrives. This relates to an old Icelandic habit of eating from lidded bowls that were stored on the floor, often under the bed. Bowl Licker would wait until someone had finished eating for the night and retired to bed, then he would lick the inside of the bowls.

The seventh visitor was Door Slammer. He would arrive in the house during the night and spend the evening slamming doors, ensuring that nobody could get any rest.

The visitor on 19 December was Skyr Gobbler. Skyr is an

Icelandic dairy product similar to yoghurt. Skyr Gobbler liked it so much he would sneak into the pantry and stuff himself with it until he was rolling in agony and fit to burst as a result of his own gluttony.

Next came Sausage Swiper. By now you've probably got the gist of how this works, but his trick of choice was to steal all the sausages from the household and eat them for himself.

The 21st saw a break from food-stealing as Window Peeper arrived. Window Peeper was principally a voyeur who enjoyed staring through windows and eyeing up what was inside. However, he wasn't averse to stealing any children's toys that seemed particularly appealing. If a child looked through the window and saw Window Peeper staring back, the Yule Lad would make faces to terrify the child until he was left alone to go about his business.

Door Sniffer arrived on 22 December. He hid behind doors, and used his huge nose to sniff out cake and bread, which he would steal for himself.

The next day was St Thorlak's Day and this was the day the traditional Icelandic Christmas dish of smoked lamb would be cooked. It is perhaps unsurprising therefore that the day's new arrival would be Meat Hook, who would use a cunningly constructed hook to reach down the chimney and attempt to winch the meat outside so he could devour it himself.

Lastly, Christmas Eve saw a visit from Candle Beggar. Before the widespread use of electricity, candles tended to be fairly expensive and it was a rare treat for a child to be given his or her own candle. Candle Beggar's goal was to find children who had been given candles and pinch one for himself.

Although this rendition is now the accepted version of the Yule Lads' mythology, originally the number and order of the

Yule Lads who visited fluctuated from town to town and from teller to teller, and there were countless other Yule Lads who were added and embellished within different households, all with their own unique characteristics. By the middle of the eighteenth century they had supplanted their mother Grýla as many parents' preferred choice of threat to coerce their children into behaving. And, as a device to silence bored children on a long, dull winter night, the Yule Lads were an unqualified success; they were known throughout the country as an effective scare tactic to terrify children into good behaviour, and parents found they could persuade their children to comply with any demand for good behaviour by assuring them a rather unpleasant visitor would be the consequence of disobedience.

There is no clear record of the psychological effects of such threats but it clearly became a major issue, for in 1746 a public decree was issued that 'the foolish custom of scaring children with the Yuletide lads and ghosts'.[19]

It is tempting to see this as an early attempt at state welfare intervening to save children from mental abuse and scarring wrought by strict parents. The truth however is that religion, rather than child welfare, was the more likely motivating force. Iceland was firmly under the influence of Pietism at the time. Pietism was a strictly devout form of Lutheranism and, as such, strongly opposed to any form of mythology or celebration that wasn't wholly Christian in origin. Therefore the ban on the Yule Lads was far more likely to have been actuated by religious objections to the mythological ogres' lack of relevance to Christian teachings than by sympathy for traumatised children.

It seems possible that the decree had some effect, as the Yule Lads faded in the popular imagination over the next hundred years and the stories that persist were inclined to focus on the playful, mischief-making side of their nature. The more vicious characters disappeared from the Yule Lads' canon, with the role of gobbling up of children left to Grýla. For a while it seemed that children in Iceland could sleep easy at last. This impression did not last long – for the nineteenth century brought a new terror in the form of perhaps Iceland's most terrifying Christmas creature yet. From nowhere there appeared a beast more ferocious than Grýla and more fiendish than all the Yule Lads combined. For all of a sudden, the children of Iceland lived in fear of . . .

. . . the Christmas Cat.

Jólakötturinn

At first glance, the Christmas Cat seems a far more appealing and safer prospect than an evil old hag who gobbles you alive or mischievous ogres who break into your homes with bloodthirsty intentions. Cats are, of course, hugely popular creatures and most people's gut reaction to the possibility of an attack by a Christmas cat might be a whimsical image of someone being licked to death by an unbearably cute, fluffy little kitten in a custom-made Santa hat. It might be hard to imagine, therefore, quite how Jólakötturinn, as the Christmas Cat is known in Icelandic, manages to strike fear into the hearts of children (and perhaps even adults) all over the country.

Jólakötturinn seems to be a relatively recent invention, with the first written accounts of it only appearing in the nineteenth century. Soon after its appearance it became associated with existing Icelandic Christmas mythology, assuming the role of the family pet of Grýla, Leppalúði and the Yule Lads. It is perhaps unsurprising, given the company it was keeping, that the Christmas Cat was no ordinary household moggy. In fact, despite his benign name, the Christmas Cat was a huge, ferocious beast who prowled around Iceland, creeping into people's homes and gobbling up children come Christmas Day.

Worse still, the Christmas Cat differed in one key respect from Grýla, the Yule Lads and other terrifying European Christmas figures such as the Krampus and Zwarte Piet; with all of those creatures the child had control over their own destiny. True, Grýla or the Krampus might prey on the naughty, but the child still knew that, just so long as he or she resisted temptation and did what they were told, they would surely be safe and would live another year.

Not so with the Christmas Cat. This was a creature that did not differentiate between the well-behaved child and the naughty one. Children knew that even a year of virtue and kind acts could not guarantee the Christmas Cat would leave them in peace come Christmas Day.

That is not to say the cat was indiscriminate in its targets. In actual fact, every child knew what would keep them safe from the Christmas Cat; the Christmas Cat would only eat those who received no new clothes for Christmas. But of course, this was something out of the child's control. However much they begged, however much they pleaded, however much they cajoled their parents, ultimately a lapse of memory or act of negligence from their parents could see the child end up as the cat's meal.

So, in the days preceding Christmas, the child would face an anxious wait to find out whether their parents had done what was necessary to ensure they could survive Christmas and get through to the spring intact. Any clothing, no matter how small and insignificant, would do. But the child knew that, without it, they were sure to die in the cat's claws.

The story of the Christmas Cat is unusual, and perhaps even unique, insofar as, whilst most Christmas and Yule figures across almost all cultures punish those who are judged to be naughty and thus, on some level, have merited that punishment, here it is an innocent and giftless child that suffers. What's more, clearly there is a social bias at work here, for it seems to be a mythology that's heavily biased in favour of wealthy families who can easily afford to clothe and feed their children. Due to their riches and privilege, these people will be able to give the child what they need to survive the winter, whilst a poor person, who perhaps genuinely cannot afford to clothe their family, risks having a child taken away from them in a brutal and deeply traumatic way.

Whilst this certainly seems cruel and unfair, it also reflects an unfortunate reality that it was likely to be the poor and under-clothed, and particularly children (as well as the elderly), who were the most likely to succumb to the ravages of winter. And perhaps this is the reason why the myth of the Christmas Cat perhaps possessed more power as a metaphor than the Yule Lads or Grýla. It is true that children may well have wandered into danger without the threat of fearsome ogres lurking in the forest waiting to punish their misdeeds, and there was a life-preservation aspect to the fear of these sinister figures. Nonetheless, they were as much a threat for ensuring discipline, conformity to expectations and avoidance of any behaviour that angered parents as they were an instruction to ensure survival. The Christmas Cat, on the other hand, represented the terror of a real, specific threat that the winter would bring.

In actuality, there was a moral lesson in the story of the

Christmas Cat, but it was one that parents, rather than children, were to follow. In the nineteenth century the most important aspect of Christmas preparations in Iceland was to do all the work necessary to be ready for Christmas and, by extension, the middle of winter. This included cleaning the house and preparing candles from sheep-droppings. The act of giving everyone in the family a candle for Christmas in the nineteenth century was the earliest form of Christmas gift-giving in Iceland. A child would be excited to receive their first (and probably only) candle of the year and, given the dark conditions and poor lighting offered by lamps of the time, the effect of the whole family lighting their candles in unison would have been a magical experience. As we saw above, the Yule Lads too saw the value of the candles and Candle Beggar would try to steal them, so a candle was a precious thing indeed.

However, the most important preparation of all was the knitting or spinning of clothes, which was important both for keeping families warm (few had the money to purchase their own) and for taking to the local shop to exchange for food and essentials, plus, if someone had knitted particularly well, luxuries for Christmas. The story of the Christmas Cat, therefore, existed to remind families (and especially mothers, who would do the knitting and spinning) of the importance of spinning all the thread and knitting all the wool in time to get it to the shops and, of course, to clothe their children for the winter months. Thus the Christmas Cat does in fact punish misbehaviour (and specifically laziness or failure to prioritise tasks), but it is the parent who is threatened with the punishment of losing their child rather than the children themselves – not that this would be much comfort to the child taken away and eaten.

There is a second way to read the story of the Christmas Cat and that's as a parable of collective responsibility, for it also serves as a reminder to the wealthy, and perhaps pertinently to their children in the formative years of education and a growing understanding of the world, of the mortal threat posed to poor children in the wintertime. The story demonstrates to the affluent that people who are less fortunate and privileged than they are might well find themselves in peril in the wintertime without help from those who can afford to give it. In this sense, the threat of the Christmas Cat acts a trigger for the wealthy to give clothes and supplies to the poor and to encourage charitable giving. This is a more modern reading of the Christmas Cat which has some currency in Iceland today, but unfortunately there is not much evidence to suggest it was a particularly successful tool for mobilising charitable actions back in the nineteenth century.

Into the Twentieth Century

One of the biggest reasons why the stories of the Yule Lads and the Christmas Cat are remembered today is the popularity of the written word in Iceland, due to its high literacy rates, and specifically a collection of poems called *Jólin Koma* ('Christmas Has Come') by the Icelandic poet Jóhannes úr Kötlum. Primarily a political writer and campaigner, *Jólin Koma* was unusual for Kötlum in being a book of poems for children, but reflected his patriotism and desire to record Icelandic traditions in order to preserve them for future generations.

The volume was a huge success throughout Iceland, and its effect on the Yule Lads and the Christmas Cat was comparable to the effect Clement Clarke Moore's 'The Night Before Christmas' had on the American Santa Claus after its publication in 1823. Just as Santa's habit of sneaking down the chimney, his sleigh and the names of his reindeer and even – through Moore's description and Thomas Nast's later illustration of the poem – Santa's appearance were established universally as a result of Moore's work, so Kötlum's poetry produced a nationally agreed image and version of the tales of both the Yule Lads and the Christmas Cat.

Indeed, the commonly accepted description of the Yule Lads and their activities stems directly from Kötlum, and his rendering of the names of the thirteen Yule Lads and their roles is now widely seen as the 'official' account of the myth and is the version celebrated in Iceland today.

Much like the fairytales of the Brothers Grimm, the playful but macabre tone of Kötlum's poetry has made it a popular feature of Icelandic childhoods ever since its publication. Kötlum's poem on Jólakötturinn the Christmas Cat captures the ferocity of the beast and the terror the creature inspired, and the poem has even been set to music and recorded by the popular Icelandic singer Björk.

Unfortunately, the poem has never been officially translated into English. However, I have attempted to create my own version of the poem that, whilst not quite a literal translation of the original, hopefully captures the message, spirit and tone of Kötlum's original work.[20]

The Christmas Cat
Based on 'Jólakötturinn' by Jóhannes úr Kötlum

Everyone knows the Christmas Cat,
He's angry, huge and mean,
But nobody knows where he came from
Or where he will next be seen.

BAD SANTAS

His eyes stared at you, open wide,
Both of them fierce ablaze,
It took a brave, brave man indeed
To steadily meet his gaze.

His whiskers were like razors,
His back was curved up high,
And those sharp claws on his hairy paws
Could make a grown man cry.

He curled and curved his great big tail,
He jumped and scratched and hissed,
Sometimes by the harbourside,
Sometimes in the mountain mist.

Vicious, large and evil,
Through freezing snows he came,
And in the houses everywhere
Folk trembled at his name.

A cruel 'meow' would let you know
Something evil was on its way,
And mice were never meat enough,
Men were his natural prey.

He feasted on the very poor
Who worked the Christmas through,
But still had no new clothes to wear
No coat, no shirt, no shoe.

He'd steal their Christmas dinner,
He'd eat it with one chew,
And because their dinner was so small
He would then eat them too.

So mothers sat at spinning wheels,
They span their wool and thread
To make some clothes to give their child
So the Cat would not strike them dead.

But if a child received no new clothes
The threat was very real,
When the Cat made his Christmas call
They'd become his Christmas meal.

Candlelight on Christmas Eve,
The Cat peers through the pane,
Sees children clad in new costume,
Knows his efforts are in vain.

Perhaps a shirt, perhaps some socks,
A vest, a scarf, or shoe,
Whatever the child needed
To see the winter through.

The Cat would sigh, would hiss, would howl,
It would beat his mighty paws,
But there was no more he could do,
For the child stayed out of his claws.

I'm not sure he's still around,
Nobody I know can say,
But if we all get Christmas clothes
That Cat will be kept at bay.

If you see a child who's going cold,
Garments ragged and threadbare,
Help save him from the Christmas Cat,
Give him something new to wear.

This good deed will keep them safe
And give you a warm feeling too,
It will give you joy throughout your day
And a happy Christmas too.

The poems gained both the Christmas Cat and the Yule Lads a resurgence of popularity and this has continued into the twenty-first century. However, as the years wore on, something strange began to happen to the Yule Lads. Suddenly, the mischievous ogres began to change in both behaviour and appearance. Almost all trace of their past lives as violent, evil, inhuman brutes started to disappear and they began to turn into jolly old men with white beards, albeit ones that retained a childlike sense of fun. Whereas once they'd appeared in traditional Icelandic clothes, they now began to wear red suits with a white trim, black boots, black belt and red hat with a fur trimming. And what was more, although they continued their pranks, such as candle-stealing, sausage-swiping and pan-licking, they also began to show a more generous side, for any child who left a shoe out each night that a Yule Lad arrived would receive a small gift from the Yule Lads (unless, of course, the child had misbehaved too much, in which case they would receive a raw potato). All of a sudden, it seemed that the Yule Lads had, in effect, become Santa Claus.

This change has not gone unnoticed and it has caused some concern amongst traditionalists who are keen to preserve Iceland's unique Christmas heritage. Since 1999 the National Museum of Iceland has been actively seeking a new national image for the Yule Lads, more in keeping with Icelandic tradition and less reminiscent of that of Santa Claus, and the Yule Lads now visit the museum each Christmas clad in more traditional costumes of wool, felt and sheepskin.

Despite not being completely immune to the globalisation of Christmas and the gradual spread of Christmas mythology, Iceland nonetheless retains its curious and wonderful traditions as strongly as any country in the world. Whilst perhaps no clearer example exists of how fearsome Christmas nightmares eventually became benign seasonal gift-givers, the Yule Lads still retain the majority of their unique characteristics. Meanwhile, the threat of Grýla lives on, even if she doesn't strike quite as much terror as she did back at her peak in the seventeenth century. And still today, children lie awake at Christmas Eve praying both that they will receive new clothes for Christmas and that the sinister meowing they can hear in the distance is merely the product of their imagination.

6

Scatological Traditions

The Caganer and Tió de Nadal (Spain)

This is a book that's supposed to be about Christmas but so far I've spent a lot of time talking about people getting maimed, dismembered or bloodily murdered by feral winter beasts. The long winter nights might have conjured terrible beasts out of people's imaginations but surely there has to be more to Christmas traditions than being ripped to shreds by wild monsters?

Indeed there does. Catalonia has a tradition that does not involve demons or blood or evil trolls or pagan rituals in animal masks but simply recreating the scene of the birth of the baby Jesus with a host of traditional characters – the baby himself, Mary, Joseph, the Wise Men, the angels, the shepherds and the animals. And, of course, the defecating peasant.

The caganer, to give the defecating peasant his correct name, is a unique and amusing tradition that began in Catalonia sometime around the eighteenth century but has appeared in parts of Spain, Portugal and Italy too. He is a figurine who features in nativity scenes and is traditionally dressed in a white shirt, black trousers and a red hat. And as the name suggests, he is always shown squatting with his trousers around his ankles and a large, brown stool curled up behind him.

Usually the caganer is a small, subtle figure. He is rarely placed prominently in the scene but is almost always hidden away in a corner. Children will make a game of trying to spot him. However, in 2010 the Maremagnum shopping centre in Barcelona broke a Guinness World Record with their Christmas display of a 19ft-tall caganer. This meant that three storeys' worth of shoppers could enjoy spectacular views of a giant man taking a dump as they went around buying their Christmas gifts.

Where Does the Caganer Come from?

The origin of the caganer is not clear but numerous theories exist. Perhaps the most plausible of these is that the Catalans of the eighteenth century felt nativity scenes had become too fantastical, too idealised and too detached from reality. Nativity scenes had become so stale that they had lost all sense of what it means to be human. People wanted to challenge this and chose to insert the most bluntly realistic human image they could think of – a man relieving himself.

The theory goes that this is all about social equality. Crude though he might be, the caganer is only doing something that all of us do every day, and his presence at the nativity serves as a reminder to forget our airs and graces and accept the fundamental similarities between us all.

Furthermore, in showing us himself before the Lord Jesus in perhaps the most humiliating state possible, the caganer demonstrates humility and human weakness; reminding people that even the flawed and the sinners have their place in Jesus's world. The caganer merely tries, in the crudest form possible, to remind us who we really are.

Yet another theory is both quite sweet and completely disgusting. It is the idea that the peasant had no money, no gold, no frankincense and no myrrh to offer the baby Jesus so has decided to share his faeces with the Lord as it is literally the only thing he owns.

Alternatively the caganer may be a symbol of the results of

Christmas overindulgence – or perhaps it may just have been that somebody thought it was funny to stick a defecating man in a Christmas scene!

There are also claims that the caganer is a nod to pagan traditions of days gone by, specifically to belief in the importance of encouraging crop growth. By defecating, the caganer is actually fertilising the Earth for the New Year; perhaps farmers who did not put a caganer in their nativity scene were doomed to a poor crop the following year.

Celebrity Defecation

These days the caganer does not have to be a peasant. In recent years, demand has risen for 'celebrity defecators' – models of popular figures of sport, politics, stage and screen all literally caught with their trousers down: politicians from Vladimir Putin to Fidel Castro to Barack Obama; sports stars from Lionel Messi to Rafa Nadal to Lewis Hamilton; musicians from Mick Jagger to Michael Jackson to Bruce Springsteen. Caganers exist of all of them engaged in defecating, even the Dalai Lama, Ghandi and Albert Einstein. Apparently Queen Elizabeth II is a particularly popular December defecator.

This is probably quite bemusing for the people depicted, but caganer-makers see using someone's image as a celebrity caganer as an honour and a positive acknowledgement of respect. After all, as Oscar Wilde very nearly said, 'The only thing worse than being so famous that there is a figurine made of you defecating is not being so famous that there is a figurine made of you defecating.'

Perhaps unsurprisingly, the pooing peasant is not universally popular. Religious traditionalists feel he detracts from the holiness of the nativity scene. The Catalan Capuchin monk and author Father Basili Di Rubi felt that the caganer was not only in bad religious taste but was simply aesthetically unpleasant to look at. The Franco regime tried to crack down on the caganer as a symbol of Catalan nationalism. In 2005 the authorities in Barcelona wanted to leave the caganer out of Christmas scenes for a different reason – they were trying to clean up the image of the city and worried that the caganer encouraged people to defecate in public. There was a subsequent wave of protest from Catalans who were proud of their Christmas crapper. The authorities ultimately relented and the caganer remains.

Tió de Nadal

You might think that having a Christmas tradition based around defecation is slightly unusual. But how about having two Christmas traditions based around defecation? For the caganer is not the only scatological tradition that the Catalans enjoy. There is also the Tió de Nadal – a rather unique Catalan Christmas log.

In fact, the Tió de Nadal gives the phrase 'Christmas log' a whole new meaning. It is, as you might assume, a hollow piece of wood. Originally this would have been a simple log but these days it is commercially produced and often has a pair of forearms, a cartoon face and a traditional Catalan hat. The log sits in or near the fireplace from around 8 December and, rather than being burned on the fire like a normal log, it is covered with a blanket to keep it warm. Children are encouraged to be kind to the log and to feed it and treat it well. And children know they have to follow this instruction – for the Tió de Nadal is actually a highly unusual festive gift-giver and children know that the kindness they show to their festive log will lead to them being rewarded with presents. So children offer food to the log, placing it on or underneath the blanket. By the next morning the parents have taken the food and the children find that it has 'mysteriously' disappeared.

Finally, on Christmas Day – or sometimes Christmas Eve – the ceremony of the Tió de Nadal begins. The children are given a stick and are encouraged to beat the log repeatedly whilst singing the songs of Tió de Nadal, which crudely implore the log to excrete presents for the family.

The songs tend to have translations that involve slightly unusual language for a children's ceremony.

For example:

Shit log, shit me a gift
Shit me turrón* and shit me sweets,
If you don't shit well,
I'll hit you with a stick, shit log!

Upon hearing the song, and on being beaten repeatedly, the log will excrete one gift at a time. These are usually small treats such as sweets and chocolate that the parents have concealed inside the log or under the blanket. The adult reaches under the blanket and 'finds' what the Tió de Nadal has excreted. A great play is made of the effort the log has gone to in order to produce the gift, and then the next child (if there is more than one) takes their turn to beat the log and chant for a gift to be 'shat' out. And so on and so on until there are a number of sweets and chocolates for the family to share.

The ceremony ends when the log no longer produces sweets

---

* A Spanish delicacy similar to nougat.

but instead excretes something sharper – usually a herring or a bulb of garlic. This means the log has run dry for the year and the ceremony is over.

Usually the Tió de Nadal only produces small gifts such as sweets and chocolates. There are larger presents but they don't come from the Christmas log, or for that matter from Saint Nicholas[*] or even Santa Claus, but instead from the first of all festive gift-givers in Christian belief – the Three Kings. Because it was said that the Three Kings arrived on 6 January to give presents to the baby Jesus, it is now claimed in Spain that they also come on the eve of 6 January to give gifts to all the children.

Much like the celebration of St Nicholas's arrival in the Netherlands, the arrival of the Three Kings is a public event. They arrive by boat on 5 January, and that evening there is a big festival with floats, bands and a carnival procession. Also, much like the St Nicholas traditions, children leave their shoes out overnight on 5 January, and the following morning the Three Kings have brought them gifts.

The Three Kings' procession is a hugely popular event in Spain but, as is the case everywhere else, US films and television shows have brought Santa Claus into wider public consciousness and led to awkward questions from children. There is also a growing tradition of bigger presents being given out by the Tió de Nadal in recent times, which has created a situation where some Catalan parents feel pressured by the presence of a trio of gift-givers, and some children get presents three times over.

The official origin of Three Kings' Day is that in 1885 the

* Even though the Dutch claim he comes from Spain.

Spanish Government called for an annual parade to honour the Three Wise Men. However, Clement A. Miles, who studied Christmas traditions around Europe in the early twentieth century, reports that a tradition in Madrid already existed where men would go out with pots and pans and make as much noise as possible. A procession travelled around the city whilst some men carried a ladder, with one of them mounting it occasionally, climbing to the top to see if he could see the Three Kings coming. Miles speculates that this might originally have been a pre-Christian rite based around scaring away the Devil or evil spirits. If so, it would suggest that perhaps the Spanish Government sanctioned an official celebration as a means of phasing out its noisy and unchristian predecessor.

Similar rituals, with the aim of warding away evil on Twelfth Night, have existed elsewhere in Europe. After all, the twelve days of Christmas had seen the dead, the demonic and damned free to wander where they wanted, and somebody had to make sure that they left again.

In parts of Switzerland young men would form a similar procession to the one in Madrid, with torches, lanterns, horns, bells and pretty much anything that made a sound that would terrify local spirits. In the eastern Alps there was a similar procession called Berchtenlaufen, where armed boys charged through the streets shouting wildly to ward off evil. A similar event in Labruguière saw the town's inhabitants rushing through the streets making disconcordant sounds. Nuremberg has a tradition of Bergnacht, which involved youths running through the town on Epiphany Eve, hammering on doors to annoy the spirits and encourage them to leave. It probably had pretty much the same effect on the people of Nuremberg. Meanwhile, in Greece, priests would spend Epiphany travelling around the local houses and blessing them all with holy water to rid the towns of Kallikantzoroi for another year.

With the forces of evil thwarted, Christmas celebrations were put to bed and the festival was over for another year. So there is more to Christmas traditions than being ripped to shreds by wild monsters. Just not a whole lot more!

7

Organised Chaos

The Lord of Misrule (England)

The Epiphany was an important day in the Christian calendar. It marked both the arrival of the Wise Men and the last of the twelve days of Christmas. Before the Industrial Revolution, people tended not to work much during the twelve days – indeed, for an agricultural society in the middle of winter, there was not much work to be done. Christmas really was a twelve-day festival and Epiphany was its climax. As such, people liked to end the holiday with a bang and 6 January was a huge celebration. Nowadays we think of Christmas parties in terms of alcohol, debauchery, outrageous behaviour, drunkenly offending your social superiors and a head full of regret the following day. However, it's important not to judge the past by today's standards.

Because 500 years ago Epiphany parties were much, much worse.

The Bean King and the Pea Queen

Up until the seventeenth century, Christmas celebrations centred around the suspension of the social rules and customs that governed society. It was a time of role-reversals where prevailing conventions were forgotten. The devout were permitted to relax and enjoy themselves, and feudal lords might invite peasants to dine with them. Priests were permitted to take a break from religious solemnity and engage in the pranks and boisterous behaviour denied to them the rest of the year.

Even against the backdrop of this apparent spirit of egalitarianism, the rich still found ways to assert themselves. Kings and queens demanded financial contributions from the lords who served them, and the feudal landlords expected a gift of extra produce from their peasants. While such gifts were not strictly compulsory, there would be an implied threat of harsh treatment for anyone who failed to hand them over.

Nonetheless, there were also practices that, at least in theory, challenged the status quo. One tradition at Twelfth Night parties in the Middle Ages was to bake a fruitcake with a pea and a bean secreted within it. Whoever found the bean would be declared the 'Bean King' and whoever found the pea would be the 'Pea Queen'. The pair would then rule the household for the night, giving out orders and demanding reverence and worship from the rest of the party. Provided nobody cheated, this was an egalitarian celebration where servants could get to order their masters around and children might even become the rulers of their own parents. Although this tradition has now died out in England, versions of it still exist elsewhere in the world. France has two types of 'Kings' cake' – *galette des Rois* in the north and *tortell des Rois* in the south. Spain has a Kings' cake called the *rosca de reyes* and Portugal has the *bola rei*. With many of these traditions, there is hidden a figurine to determine who is the king of festivities and a bean to decide who pays for the cake.

The Feast of the Holy Innocents

The possibility of getting to boss around their parents by becoming the Bean King was a rare glimpse of power for children. Otherwise, Christmas traditions were not really geared towards them. The idea of Christmas being a time for children and families is largely an invention of the Victorian Age. Three hundred years before that, children generally got pushed to the side in the drunken debauchery of adult Christmas celebrations. True, children in many parts of Europe were visited by St Nicholas or his assistants and they might get some sweets if they were good, but even then the whole ritual of St Nicholas was designed around making them behave, rather than rewarding or spoiling them. What's more, the gifts for good behaviour were tempered with beatings for misbehaviour – perhaps even more severe than the ones they might get the rest of the year – if they failed the tests St Nicholas set them.

Happily, England was an exception to this, and I am relieved to say that my ancestors were not so brutal as to set young children spurious tests on religion and then ritually beat them if they didn't know the answers. Instead, the English just skipped the formalities and ritually beat the children anyway.

These beatings took place on 28 December, a day known as Childermass or the Feast of the Holy Innocents. In the nativity story, this was the day when King Herod – terrified by the threat of the 'newly crowned King' – ordered that all newborn males in the local area be murdered. Perhaps understandably, it was seen as an unlucky day in the Christian calendar. In England, it was said that any wedding that took place on 28 December would be doomed to disaster, and it was considered unlucky to conduct business of any kind on that day. Many people believed that whichever day of the week Childermass fell on would be unlucky for the whole of the following year.

But Childermass was still most unlucky of all for the children. For up until around the seventeenth century, it was believed that ritually beating a child with a stick at Childermass brought the beater good luck and reminded the child of both King Herod's viciousness and Jesus's suffering.

This might sound odd – and I am pleased to say that there seems to be no evidence of this ritual surviving anywhere in England today. However, ritually beating people up at Christmas was more common than you might think.

In Catholic areas of Germany, there was a tradition called *pfeffern* where children were entitled to beat their parents with a stick and demand gifts or sweets. In France, as in England, children were whipped on Holy Innocents' Day, but only if they stayed in bed too long. In Wales the last person in the family to get out of bed on Boxing Day was beaten with sticks and made to act as the family servant for the day, and in the ever-egalitarian Sweden the first person to wake up on Christmas Eve would collect twigs and hand them round to the family so that everyone could whip each other.

In the Czech Republic the whippings continue to this day, but they happen at Easter rather than Christmas and take the form of a surrealist valentine. Teenage boys turn up at the houses of girls they fancy, whip them with the branches and – sometimes – a group of boys will seize a girl and throw her into a bathtub. The girl's mother will then give the boys money for showing their daughter favour. You might assume this is a tradition that the boys appreciate far more than the girls but my Czech correspondent assures me that girls feel disappointed if nobody turns up to whip them.

It is not entirely clear why walloping people with sticks was such a popular pastime in medieval times, but it may have its roots in a Roman festival called Lupercalia. This was not a midwinter festival (it actually took place over three days around what is now Valentine's Day) but it did involve men running through the streets with no clothes on, dishing out whippings to any women they passed. According to the Greek historian Plutarch, this was supposed to bring good luck.

> Many of the noble youths and of the magistrates run up and down through the city naked, for sport and laughter striking those they meet with shaggy thongs. And many women of rank also purposely get in their way, and like children at school present their hands to be struck, believing that the pregnant will thus be helped to an easy delivery, and the barren to become pregnant.[21]

Saturnalia and Kalends

Whipping people was not the only Christmas custom said to have come from Roman festivals. The medieval rituals around social equality, as well as the drunken parties and costume-wearing associated with the Christmas season, were said to be influenced by two Roman festivals – Saturnalia and the January Kalends.

Saturnalia was a festival honouring Saturn, the god of the harvest. Like Kekri, it was a festival that originally took place in the autumn, but it eventually became a midwinter celebration from 17 to 23 December. The Kalends of January festivities followed a few days later and ran from 1 to 5 January. Between the two of them they spanned what is now the Christmas season.

Like the medieval Christmas, Saturnalia was a festival that involved abandonment of the usual social rules. Social hierarchies were forgotten and people of all classes mingled together as equals. Gambling (usually illegal in Roman society) was permitted and the masters would give their slaves a banquet. The streets were full of singing, partying, Saturnalia greetings and novelty gifts. In later periods of Saturnalia, a slave or person of low social status was appointed the king of festivities. He was free to order people to do as he pleased and they had to obey. This could be seen as a clear predecessor of England's Lord of Misrule, which we will come to shortly.

As the Greek writer Lucian of Samosota put it in around AD 150, becoming the king of the festivities meant that 'you can not only escape silly orders but can give them yourself, telling one man to shout out something disgraceful about himself, another to dance naked, pick up the flute-girl and carry her three times around the house'.[22]

The Kalends actually began the night before 1 January, when there was a wild procession and celebration through the streets, without the moral reprobation that such exuberance would usually bring – essentially a precursor to modern New Year's Eve celebrations. Then there were five days of customary celebration. On the first day the authorities would hand out money to the people. On the second day people would stay at home, playing dice and engaging in festivities where, like Saturnalia, the powerful would act as slaves to the weak. The third was a day of public races and then there were two more days of celebration before the festival drew to a close.

The festival also involved people dressing in costumes and holding street parties, and Asterius, the Bishop of Amasea in Roman Turkey in around 400 AD, claimed chaos and anarchy reigned supreme. Farmers selling goods in towns would be jeered at and spanked, and town officials would be pestered by the public into handing over money. Soldiers, freed from military discipline for the festive season, would both impersonate and seduce women. Children would go from house to house selling fruit covered in tinsel, for which they would receive expensive items in exchange. Asterius was not a fan of Kalends. He found it ungodly, rowdy and over-commercial and complained that it conditioned children to expect material goods rather than to appreciate spiritual pleasures.[23] You suspect he'd be even less impressed by the modern Christmas.

The parallels between these Roman festivals and Christmas are easy enough to spot but, much like the Wild Hunt, trying to prove a link between the two is harder than you might expect. Officially at least, Saturnalia was not celebrated into the Christian era. As early as the fourth century it had largely been merged into Christian Christmas celebrations and then fallen out of fashion. The traditions had spread around Europe and may have continued unofficially but there is no certain evidence to prove this. The US religious historian Max Harris claims the traditions that influenced characters such as the Krampus and Schmutzli – wearing masks and dressing as animals – did not arise until after the advent of Christianity in the Roman Empire and might well have been the result of early Christians satirising, rather than worshipping, pagan figures. It might be that what the Church later saw as remnants of pagan worship were actually long-forgotten attempts to lampoon the pagan gods of old in the name of Christianity.

As is the case with the Wild Hunt, most of the earliest accounts of the pagan roots of Christmas are written by Christians criticising practices they disliked and wanted to abolish. Most modern accounts of the influence of Saturnalia stem from the seventeenth century, when Puritan preachers blamed the pagan influences of Saturnalia for the wild excesses of drinking, gambling and raucous behaviour. Whilst these might have had genuine pagan roots, there was a tendency amongst Christians during the Reformation to link any practice they disliked to ancient pagan worship and to accuse anyone involved with it of being in league with the Devil. Similarly, modern-day pagans have a vested interest in linking as many modern-day practices as possible to pre-Christian religions. Between the two, it is easy for the pagan roots of Christmas to be overstated.

Certainly it is hard to see how the anarchism and chaos at the heart of the Christmas celebrations of the Middle Ages directly links to Christian celebrations, but perhaps the mistake is assuming there was a holy aspect to these festivities at all – it might simply have been a party for the sake of a party, without any real religious implications. Many of the activities central to medieval Christmas celebrations – singing, drinking alcohol, dressing up in masks, raucous behaviour and giving gifts or tributes – are major ingredients of parties and carnivals across the world. This could be because of the lingering influence of pagan celebrations, but may just be because people link these things with having a good time.

This was not simply about getting drunk and having a party – it was also about the need for a release from the dreadfulness of the winter conditions. Nor can this need for a respite be separated from the massive social inequality and miserable quality of life that feudal peasants endured. The egalitarianism of the Christmas season, artificial though it may have been, was not only a way of allowing the powerful and respected to relax without risking disgrace but also a way of giving the worst off in society a break from being trodden underfoot by the elite. Perhaps this made their treatment the rest of the year a little more palatable and therefore helped ensure social harmony in a deeply divided society.

Whatever the origins of the celebrations, it is certainly true that medieval Britain, like ancient Rome, celebrated the middle of winter with the abandonment of rules and social status and an equality born out of chaos.

The Boy Bishop and the Feast of Fools

The Church had their own ritual involving the inversion of social hierarchy. All across western Europe cathedrals would elect a boy bishop. His role was pretty much exactly what the name suggests. He was a pubescent choirboy who was elected at the beginning of December and then dressed in full bishop's robes, and equipped with a mitre and crosier. He acted as the head of the Church from 6 December until 28 December. He performed the role of a priest, took all services apart from Mass and was free to direct church proceedings and appoint other choristers to act as his canons. The boy bishop was not universally popular – largely because traditionalists felt that the practice of having a small boy pretend to be a bishop undermined the solemnity of the Church. There were practical problems too. The congregation did not seem to take the boy bishop very seriously and members of the congregation would throw things at him or pull pranks to disrupt the services. Occasionally the boy bishops took themselves far too seriously and houses near the church would suddenly be confronted with a menacing gang of choirboys dressed as bishops and canons demanding the householders hand over money in order to absolve their sins!

The boy bishop was often associated with the Feast of Fools, a church celebration that priests would engage in during medieval times. The Feast may have originated in Turkey in the ninth century, but it became most popular in France during the twelfth century, although Britain, Scotland and many other countries observed it too. Like Saturnalia, the Feast of Fools was a relaxation of social rules within the Church and, as such, it was the time when priests and clergymen could kick back and, for a brief period, succumb to some of the temptations they had to reject for the rest of the year.

In 1445 religious scholars in France complained about the behaviour of priests during the Feast of Fools. Amongst other things, they accused the priests of wearing 'monstrous visages at the hours of office', dancing 'in the choir dressed as women, panderers or minstrels', gambling, singing 'wanton songs' and 'infamous performances with indecent gestures and verses scurrilous and unchaste'.[24] It seems some priests really knew how to let their hair down!

Shocking though this sounds, it is worth considering two points. Firstly, this letter was written by scholars who were keen to see the Feast of Fools celebrations banned. As a cursory look at modern tabloids or a quick read of Twitter will attest, it is not at all unusual for people expressing moral outrage to exaggerate the scale or extent of a problem, and it is likely that, if the above events happened, the worst excesses were confined to a minority of priests and a minority of churches.

Secondly, for all the moral authority they were compelled to display, priests and clergymen were ordinary people, often peasants or from the lower classes. The pressure to suddenly present themselves as morally upstanding, learned authorities on spiritual matters was most likely very difficult to take, as was the need to abstain from vice, sin and temptation. It might be that those few days of relaxation from the pressures to act in a 'holy' manner were essential to a priest's mental wellbeing.

One of the stranger traditions of the Feast of Fools was the

145

Feast of the Ass. This involved a service where a donkey was led into church and tied to the altar whilst the priests and the congregation sang a Latin hymn with a refrain that sounded like a donkey braying. This was a homage to the donkey who carried Mary and the baby Jesus into Egypt to escape Herod's wrath. It is unclear how many priests took it as a heartfelt tribute and how many just thought it was fun to impersonate a braying donkey.

The religious scholars saw the Feast of Fools as a sacrilegious ceremony that undermined and mocked the Church from within and allowed priests to flirt with paganism and satanic rituals under God's own roof. Nonetheless, some modern academics feel that the worst excesses of the Feast of Fools were exaggerated. Max Harris points out that the Church would not have sanctioned or tolerated the Feast of Fools for as long as it did if it really had been the anarchic bedlam that the scholars describe, and suggests that in most places the Feast of Fools consisted more of merriment than debauchery. What is certain is that, by the early fifteenth century, the voices in the French Church who were opposed to the Feast began to dominate. Jean Gerson, Chancellor of the University of Paris from around 1400, was particularly vocal in his attacks on the Feast and claimed that obscene songs, gestures and costumes were associated with priests during the feast, whose purpose was to entice Christian boys into committing sexual improprieties. It is worth noting that Gerson never claimed to have witnessed these events and acted on rumours alone.

In 1400 the Chapter of Auxerre banned priests from participating in the Feast of Fools and specified a host of activities priests were henceforth barred from. These included excessively ringing the church bells, stealing cloaks from townspeople and demanding a fee for their return, 'striking anyone'[25] or any actions that

146

discredited the Church. Rumours abounded of mischief-making priests engaging in everything from lewd behaviour, to soaking people with bucketfuls of water, to driving through the town with a cartload of cow dung and throwing it at passers-by.

During the fifteenth century there was a concerted attempt by traditionalists in the Church to abolish the Feast of Fools as a pagan practice, and this makes many of the reports of the worst aspects of the Feast of Fools extremely unreliable. It is possible that the opponents of the feast based their opposition on the terrible behaviour it encouraged, but it is equally likely that those detractors heard rumours of the Feast's supposed worst excesses and reported them as fact to add credibility to their argument. My suspicion is that the truth is somewhere in between – that some priests did use the Feast of Fools as cover for a range of malicious and cruel pranks but that these acts were nowhere near as widespread as the detractors made out.

The Lord of Misrule

Much of the real chaos of Christmas was not generated in the churches but amongst the ordinary populace. A key character in English Christmas celebrations of the Middle Ages was the Lord of Misrule. Like the Bean King and the King of Saturnalia, this was a person from the peasant classes who found himself with the power to direct festivities. Although he came to encapsulate the drunken chaos and anarchy of the Christmas period, the Lord's roots were actually rather gentrified.

Initially he was a figure who was employed by wealthy households or royal courts – in the latter it would often be the court jester taking on an additional role for the Christmas season – to direct the Christmas entertainment and ensure that the party season went smoothly. Churches would sometimes nominate an Abbot of Misrule to carry out a similar function. In both cases they would be charged with watching over the celebrations, keeping an eye on the servants and essentially acting as a combination of events manager and master of ceremonies. They also had some power to direct people during the Christmas season and would have indemnity to play practical jokes on fellow servants and their masters alike, or to instruct them to participate in games or activities for the amusement of the household. Because the Lord of Misrule knew he had to go back to being a servant two weeks later and would want to keep his job and avoid unpleasant repercussions, it is likely that most of his jokes were well-meant and would have involved harmless fun, rather than outright humiliation.

Things changed when the concept of the Lord of Misrule spread to ordinary townsfolk. At this point, the custom became much wilder and more chaotic. Christmas revellers would spill out on the streets, drinking and making merry and, perhaps spontaneously or perhaps as part of a plan, a Lord of Misrule to reign over the Feast of Fools would be elected from amongst their number.

Like his counterpart within the houses of the gentry, the Lord had the authority to direct people to do his bidding. However, the major difference was that he did not experience the tacit threat of being sacked if he told someone to do the wrong thing.

When the Lord of Misrule was in charge, it frequently led to a party on the streets that resembled a riot. The Lord had the power to command anyone to do anything he wanted, and often nobles and town leaders would have to endure humiliation and embarrassment at his hands. In theory, the mocked authority figures had to take this humiliation in good spirit, but it's hard to imagine that none of them chose to exact vengeance after the Christmas season. At the very least you would expect any Lord of Misrule who picked on a magistrate as a target would very much hope not to have any run-ins with the law over the coming year.

Perhaps for that reason – or perhaps, as with Schmutzli in Switzerland, just because of young men's desire to scare off potential sexual competition – strangers seemed to bear the brunt of the worst pranks that took place. Any merchant, farmer or traveller approaching a town to sell his wares during the Christmas period risked insults, assaults and ill-treatment. A popular prank was to identify a stranger in a long overcoat, sneak up behind him whilst he was in conversation and nail his coat to a shop door. Other favourites in the revellers' repertoire included drunkenly disrupting church services (often the ones being conducted by the boy bishops) and forming riotous bands and parading through the streets hammering impromptu home-made instruments.

Mummers and Wassailers

Very closely tied in with the Lord of Misrule was the tradition of wassailing. Wassailing basically involved a party of people going from house to house, singing folk songs and demanding food, charity or alcohol. Wassailing takes its name from a strong mulled cider and a tradition of singing songs to apple trees to encourage them to grow. It started in the Middle Ages with peasants going to sing at the house of the feudal lords and was essentially a means of the peasants begging without being seen as beggars. Tradition was that the lord would give the wassailers gifts and the wassailers would in return give their blessings and good wishes.

All of which sounds very nice. Until, of course, you come to the question of what happened if the householder didn't hand anything over. Then things could turn very unpleasant.

The most famous surviving wassail is 'We Wish You a Merry Christmas', in which the singers – in keeping with the spirit of the wassail – start off with good wishes, then demand some 'figgy pudding' (which was not all that different from Christmas pudding) before the more aggressive threats kick in.

We won't go until we've got some,
We won't go until we've got some,
We won't go until we've got some,
So bring it out here.

Nowadays this is generally sung as a comical threat, but back in the Middle Ages some landlords were doubtless terrified of the possibility of angry peasants rising up in revenge against them. This was probably a reasonable fear. Wassailers would often have been drunk and most likely held grudges against the person who demanded they pay extortionate rent and took the best of their produce. If landlords refused to give out gifts to the was-sailers, they might find themselves cursed and sworn at instead of being offered good wishes. Or they might find that their house was smashed up in retaliation – and perhaps take a beating themselves into the bargain. All told, it was probably better to hand the food and booze over.

Because of the repercussions for landlords who did not play ball with the charity-demanding peasants, wassailing gradually became associated with drunken young men engaging in acts of violence and intimidation. Nowadays the pleasant, religious side of wassailing is continued through Christmas carols, whereas the demands for gifts and threats of violence have been taken over by Hallowe'en.

Marauding through the streets causing chaos could potentially get you into a lot of trouble. Turning up at your landlord's house drunkenly demanding food and alcohol and threatening to smash up his house might get you into even more. For this reason, Christmas revellers often wanted to protect their identities.

One way which developed for them to do this was through mumming, which was basically the act of wearing a mask or costume at Christmas and either performing, partying or simply drunkenly rampaging around the neighbourhood in disguise. People would wear costumes, animal masks or dress up as the opposite sex and hold impromptu street parties, visit neighbours (or feudal lords to wassail) and generally make merry.

Although mumming and the Lord of Misrule celebrations were primarily jovial, good-natured fun, there was a darker side to the festivities. The combination of alcohol, the suspension of social rules and the anonymity of masks gave people licence to express some of the more unsavoury aspects of their personality. Many pranks of the time would have had a sadistic feel and a motive of bullying and humiliating their victims, and it is likely that women and young girls would have felt particularly uncomfortable in an atmosphere of drunken, masked men feeling they had *carte blanche* to act without repercussions.

Unsurprisingly, any specific charges of sexual misbehaviour have been lost to history but other crimes certainly happened. English folk chronicler John Brand recorded a custom in Tiverton where young men dressed up and armed themselves with swords, then used mumming as a form of blackmail to demand money and gifts; it seems unlikely that the Tivertonians were unique in this.

Eventually monarchs began to ban mumming. Henry VIII made mumming illegal and claimed that the masked marauders had been responsible for 'murders, felony, rape and other great hurts and inconveniences'.[26]

As with the Christian attempts to ban the Feast of Fools, these claims have to be taken with a pinch of salt – it is very common for people who are trying to ban a practice to highlight or exaggerate its worst aspects in order to justify their objections, and it would certainly be grossly unfair on the mummers to assume that all or most of those who took part in these events had sinister motives.

It is easy to see how the drunken, masked mobs could easily have got out of hand, though, and it is reasonable to believe there were unsavoury incidents on occasions during mumming rituals. Nonetheless, it is a bit implausible to imagine that Henry VIII – a man who slaughtered two of his wives, hoarded money from the Church and founded a new religion purely so that he could shack up with someone new whenever the mood took him – was motivated purely by ethics. Mumming's status as an unsanctioned, irreligious festival, or a humiliating mumming incident happening to someone close to the King, seem far more plausible reasons for the ban than outrage at the terrible events that took place during the festivities.

Mummers' Plays

From the eighteenth century onwards, mummers became most famous as bands of wandering actors who would travel to towns and villages or large houses to put on plays and performances and beg for money.

Mummers' plays would be spoken entirely in rhyme and verse.

There were three basic types of mummers' play but many plot features appeared in all of them.

There was the combat play – where a hero (perhaps St George) and a villain (perhaps the Dragon or a Turkish knight) would trade barbs and then fight until one of them – often the hero – was killed. A character would then lament the death and a quack doctor would emerge from the crowd for a comedy scene where they would revive the fallen warrior with a miracle cure. The hero and villain would then exchange insults again and once more fight to the death. This time the hero would triumph, and then an entirely superfluous character – perhaps Beelzebub – would turn up to perform a song, deliver a speech about the joy of Christmas and implore the audience to donate some cash to the performers.

Alternatively, there was a wooing play – a common theme would be that two or more men fancied the same woman and so would trade barbs and then fight until one of them was killed. Again, a character lamented the death and again a quack doctor would emerge from the crowd to miraculously restore the character to life. The woman would then decide she didn't want any of the men and marry the actor playing the comedy Fool. As with the combat play, a superfluous character like Beelzebub would turn up for a song and a speech about the joys of Christmas, before imploring the crowd to part with their money.

Lastly there was a sword dance. The sword dance had no plot as such, but a cast of around five characters would dance around their swords in a performance which closely resembled morris dancing. The dance would end with the 'stabbing' of one of the dancers. Luckily our good friend the quack doctor would be on hand to save him with his trusty miracle cure. Unsurprisingly, it might also then feature a performance by a superfluous character such as Beelzebub – cue song, speech and a demand for your dough. There was definitely a set pattern.

Beelzebub was not the only extraneous figure to turn up in these plays. There was also a screaming old man dressed in green and wielding a club. He would sometimes appear to extol the virtues of winter and the wonders of the festive season. He was a traditionalist who would implore people to honour these traditions and keep them alive. The man's name was sometimes given as Old Man Winter but more often he was known as Father Christmas. It's worth making a note of the name – he might be important later.

It is a widely held belief that the mummers' plays are actually a continuation of ancient pagan folk rituals, but there is very little written evidence of the plays existing prior to 1700, and it seems more likely to be a tradition which emerged after the restoration of the monarchy as a way of sanitising the mumming tradition and keeping it alive without the rowdiness and chaos it had embodied before the English Civil War.

Misrule Everywhere

Mumming traditions were by no means confined to England. Russia and many Baltic countries had similar traditions, and in Latvia mummers – often dressed as animals or living corpses – still visit houses to this day. Belarus also has a similar tradition where a group of young boys in costumes (the principal one amongst them dressed as a goat, as in Scandinavia) visits houses to sing songs of good luck in exchange for food. Mumming is also popular in Ireland, where crowds of costumed revellers called Wrenboys parade on Boxing Day carrying a wren on a stick and demanding money. St Stephen, one of the earliest Christian martyrs, was said to have been captured by the authorities after a singing wren gave away his hiding place. Up until the twentieth century the Irish would mark this by hunting and capturing a wren and parading it through the town, requesting donations from passers-by in exchange for one of the wren's feathers (and, with it, good luck). The money raised would then be used to hold a dance that evening in the town. Nowadays – probably due to animal welfare concerns – a paper wren is hidden instead of a real bird hunted.

Traditions of dressing in masks and going from home to home have also been mentioned in respect of the Krampuslaufen in Austria, the Kekripukki in Finland and Twelfth Night celebrations in parts of Spain, Germany, France and right across Europe. Carnivals in Germany and Austria from the sixteenth century frequently featured masked people challenging strangers to gamble on games of dice.

The Lord of Misrule and the traditions of anarchy were not uniquely English either. France's traditions around the Lord of Misrule are described in the opening of Victor Hugo's *The Hunchback of Notre-Dame*, which gives a detailed and vivid picture of how a fifteenth-century Epiphany play descends into anarchic chaos leading to a Feast of Fools – which, despite sharing its name with the Christian celebration, is closer in spirit to the people's celebrations around the Lord of Misrule.[27] The Pope of Fools – as the Lord is named here – is chosen by a competition to see who can pull the ugliest face, which the deformed Quasimodo wins without even trying. The party then descends to the streets and forms a drunken procession which Quasimodo unwittingly leads around the town in a march of merry chaos.

Later the drunken celebrations of the Lord of Misrule would

be taken to America. The coming centuries would see Christmas celebrations compromised in Europe as the Church dramatically changed its attitude to non-Christian midwinter celebrations, from passive tolerance to trying to cut them out completely. America was sheltered from this by the vast spaces between settlements practising different types of religious beliefs. In some areas Christmas was virtually ignored, but in others the crazed medieval celebrations would continue into the nineteenth century, until the invention of a new figure designed to counter these drunken rampages with an image of Christmas that was more friendly and child-orientated. His name was Santa Claus and we shall find out more about him later.

8

The State versus
St Nicholas

Ded Moroz (Russia)

Up until the fifteenth century there was largely a truce between Christianity and the pre-Christian folk rituals that were still widely practised. This was largely due to pragmatism – Christianity had grown as a minority religion in countries, empires and city states with other mainstream religions. From the very beginning, Christmas had been a compromise and a negotiation between Church missionaries and the pagan traditions of the people they were trying to convert. When Christianity first spread across Europe, the Church was happy to take these customs and reinterpret them to fit in with Christian beliefs, as it was a good way to convince people to at least superficially accept the new religion. For a developing religion trying to gain influence, any form of conversion was seen as a victory.

Traditional midwinter festivals were co-opted in the name of Christian festivities. Ceremonies like the Wild Hunt and rituals of thanks to the gods of the harvest were tolerated, people were allowed to dress as unholy monsters and the whole ritual of Christmas seemed to involve more drunken debauchery and tomfoolery than it did Christian worship.

Occasionally, if things got too rowdy, the Church might steer celebrations in a slightly different direction – such as pairing the wild marauders in masks with St Nicholas in order to keep them in line. But generally the Church tolerated non-Christian practices as long as their practitioners at least attended church services and called themselves Christians.

This was partly a numbers game. Christian leaders wanted as

many followers as possible – especially with the desire to get Western Europe to unite behind the Crusades. What's more, monarchs were insecure, and attempts at coups and treason were commonplace activities – the last thing kings and queens needed was a set of disgruntled soldiers who might easily transfer their loyalties to scheming leaders-in-waiting who could use the carrot of freedom from religious persecution as a lure to incite revolt.

That's not to say the Church lacked teeth – the Crusades clearly demonstrated the Popes' willingness to resort to violence to spread religion. When rogue Christian sects such as the Cathars and Waldensians rose up to challenge the authority of the Church in the twelfth century, papal inquisitions were swiftly formed to try, imprison and torture the heretics until they repented. But the Waldensians (who believed the notion of a priesthood went against the true principles of Christianity) and the Cathars (who believed the Catholics had made a terrible mistake and were inadvertently worshipping Satan rather than the 'true' God of the New Testament) were a direct challenge to the beliefs and the authority of the Catholic Church. Generally, the default position seemed to be that, so long as you left the Church alone and at least pretended to be Christian, you were free to do as you wished.

This does not mean that the Church approved of the less holy side of Christmas. It is very clear that many early priests and monks privately condemned traditions such as the Wild Hunt and the Feast of Fools. Nonetheless, the Church was still in a position where it had to pick its battles carefully, and outright confrontation or condemnation of non-Christian practices was generally avoided.

As the Church became more powerful – and perhaps as the

Church's history of piggy-backing existing celebrations was forgotten – things began to change. Clergy and priests became more disgruntled by what they saw as heathen celebrations that disregarded the Bible teachings and failed to truly honour the Word of God.

The changing status of the Church is perhaps best shown in Britain by the development of the mystery plays. Mystery plays were developed in the eleventh century when monks wrote and performed plays retelling key events from the Bible as a way to convey religious stories to the illiterate population. Unfortunately, monks quickly found they felt uncomfortable playing the more evil biblical figures, such as King Herod and the serpent of the Garden of Eden, as they deemed them unholy. So townspeople took over the plays and performed them in churchyards at Christmas and Easter. The populace were a bit less virtuous than the monks and before long began to add humour to the plays in the form of coarse language and sexual innuendo.

By the thirteenth century it had finally become too much for the clergy to take. They threw the actors out of the churchyard and began to denounce them as being – ironically for a biblical performance – unchristian. New ways had to be found to stage the plays. The townspeople built large wagons called pageants that were easy to transport, and actors acted out the plays on a two-tiered stage with scenery within the wagon. In cities like Chester and York, different city guilds would create different pageants and they would go on a procession through the town acting out the entire Bible over the course of a very long day. The clergy's reasons for rejecting these lewd interpretations of the Bible is understandable, but nonetheless the turnaround from widely tolerating non-Christian activities to condemning

THE STATE VERSUS ST NICHOLAS

(admittedly misguided) attempts to act out the Bible is a dramatic one and shows the changing status of Christianity.

Eventually the Church began to take a harder line on paganism and supposed demonic rituals than it had before. It was a gradual process but by the fifteenth century the Church would find itself waging war on paganism and all unholy beliefs. A big part of the reason for this was a growing belief in the Devil and the powers of evil. Early Christians had believed pagan practices such as magic spells and worshipping old gods to be a misguided belief in ancient superstitions, but by 1200 the Devil was a real figure to most Christians. All of a sudden, the innocent customs of costumes, animal masks and enacting ancient rituals did not seem so harmless after all.

The Black Death brought the Devil to life more than any event ever had before. Perhaps half of all Europeans died during the epidemic and something had to be blamed. In the absence of medical knowledge, it had to be either the fact that God was letting it happen to punish a people who were not religious enough or else the Devil and his minions were subverting God's will and spreading evil over the Earth.

There were a number of other reasons why Christians felt emboldened to act. Roman Catholicism had finally achieved a position as the dominant religion of western Europe and the medieval inquisitions against the Cathars and Waldensians had gone rather well. Perhaps the Church realised that it was finally in a strong enough state to take on those it deemed 'heretics' and win.

The Church now became far more vocal in trying to rid Europe of the very festivals they had previously absorbed into Christianity. Pagan traditions were savagely criticised and the Church grew stronger in its disapproval of belief in the supernatural. Witch trials had begun and those accused of witchery or heathenism were no longer merely misguided and tied to religions of the past. Now they were depicted as evil, animalistic devil-worshippers hellbent on bringing down Christianity and leading the Dark One to rise up in its place.

The fear of the Devil was contagious and this was particularly bad news for St Nicholas's menagerie of demonic assistants and equivalents. Soon dressing up as many of the Christmas creatures was frowned upon, if not banned outright. The Krampus and Perchta were banned in Austria in the seventeenth and eighteenth centuries and dressing as them was punishable by death. The Yule Lads were banned by Pietists in Iceland in the eighteenth century. In the seventeenth and eighteenth centuries the Finnish pagan festivals of Kekri and Nuut were banned by the Church. For a while people still celebrated in their barns in secret, but ultimately these festivals began to become combined with Christmas. In Sweden the presence of a tomte on your farm stopped being a sign of good luck and instead became proof that you practised witchcraft.

Other traditions struggled too. The Feast of Fools was forced out of existence, the Lord of Misrule became seen as a sinful excess and traditions of the Wild Hunt began to shift. The idea of a vast army of the dead remained a popular tradition in many parts of Europe, but Odin and Woden ceased to be associated with it. As did Christmas for that matter. Instead it was often a national hero – perhaps King Arthur in England or Holger Danske in Denmark – lying in wait with a secret army of the dead, ready to sweep in and save the day in their country's gravest hour of need.

All of a sudden, many of the cornerstones of midwinter celebrations found themselves under threat. But worse was to come –

it would not be long before the whole idea of Christmas found itself under attack.

The Reformation

As the Catholic Church became more powerful, accusations grew from inside Catholicism that the Church had lost sight of Jesus's original mission. Reformist priests such as John Wycliffe and Jan Hus attacked the church for being too rich, too hierarchical and too powerful, and Wycliffe even translated the Bible into English so that it was accessible to the common man – or it would be if education improved enough for the common man to become literate! The reformists attacked the ostentation of the churches and the luxurious life enjoyed by the Pope and the heads of the hierarchy as compared to the poverty suffered by ordinary people. They attacked the rise of traditions and practices without biblical sanction and especially the doctrine of indulgences – which had basically come to mean that pure faith alone might not get you into Heaven if you lacked the money to give to charity, but financial gifts to churches and charities could buy all sinners a get-out-of-jail-free card, no matter how terrible their crimes.

By 1517 Martin Luther had written these objections down in a letter and – at least apocryphally – nailed the letter to the door of his church, and Protestantism was born.

The history of the schism between Protestants and Catholics is violent, bloody and complicated, and the tensions between the two are still not resolved. But the upshot was that Protestants gained huge influence across Europe and had an enormous impact on the way Christmas was celebrated and, in some circumstances, whether it was celebrated at all.

One of the Protestants' biggest issues with the Catholic Church was the way saints had come to be cherished and venerated almost as much as God and Jesus. The Bible clearly stated that you should only have one God and that false idols were not to be worshipped, but many churches contained depictions of saints and many Catholics prayed directly to saints (and also the Virgin Mary) as well as to Jesus. Saints' days – including St Nicholas's Day – were a major part of the religious calendar.

Now this was not just about the demonic company that St Nicholas kept. Even St Nicholas was perceived as a problem. Martin Luther and his followers felt that the cult of St Nicholas promoted the veneration of saints and detracted from the wonder and the glory of the Lord. The fact that the celebration took place just three weeks before Christmas also meant that children's focus was on St Nicholas when the Lutherans felt it should have been Jesus's birth that was being celebrated.

At the same time, the Lutherans were pragmatists. They knew that calling for the complete abolition of a popular celebration would not endear Lutheranism to the people they wanted to convert. So they needed a way to discourage St Nicholas by replacing him with a person and a day more in keeping with Christian values. And who embodied Christian values more than Jesus Christ himself? And what better day to deliver gifts than Christmas Day?

And so it was that the Christkind – or the Christ Child – was born.

The Christkind

The Christ Child was an impressively literal creation. Quite simply, it was the baby Jesus, freshly out of his manger and clad

in white, who went round Germany and other Lutheran territories delivering gifts to children. The idea was that this was a
spiritual figure who would teach children the true meaning of
Christmas.

There were several problems with this.

The first one was a literal one. The baby Jesus was born on
Christmas Day. And delivered the presents on Christmas Eve.
This meant that, somehow or other, the baby had to either pop
out of Mary's womb pre-birth for a quick bit of gift-giving or
somehow, post-birth, travel back in time twenty-four hours and
then travel round the world handing out gifts. Before being
able to eat or speak. Even for a miracle-worker it made very little
sense.

Secondly, the whole thing was a bit hard to visualise. How on
earth does a baby deliver gifts? Between the inability to walk and
the inability to carry things, it seemed doomed from the off.

Thirdly, the whole appeal – and admittedly terror – of
Sinterklaas was that he burst into the room in full view of everyone and made a public show of bringing the gifts. Obviously
this required an adult family member or neighbour to play St
Nicholas and visit children. Clearly, the same could not happen
for the Christkind. An adult turning up dressed as a baby would
have been unconvincing and strangely unfestive. So the tradition had to be rewritten so that the Christkind appeared in the
dead of night whilst all children were asleep and delivered the
presents incognito.

Fourthly, the Lutherans made a fundamental miscalculation.
Moving the present-giving from 6 December (or the Epiphany, or
the New Year, depending on where you lived) to Christmas Day
might help increase the significance of Christmas Day but it also
increased the significance of giving presents on Christmas Day.

Ultimately, Luther's plan to popularise giving gifts at Christmas instead of at other times served to, well, popularise giving gifts at Christmas. The Lutherans basically managed to accidentally invent the very focus on the material side of Christmas that they were trying to destroy! The Christkind – or Christkindl as it was also known – also managed to give rise to the name Kris Kringle, an alternative name for Santa Claus in America.

Lastly, to a child, newborn babies can be a bit boring. They just lie there, not doing much and crying occasionally. If you offer a child a choice between a baby who turns up invisibly in the middle of the night and a man with a magnificent beard accompanied by a creature in a ferocious mask, both of them making lots of noise and trying to scare you, you'll probably find most children take the monster every time!

Perhaps people who lived under the Lutherans were lucky that they got a Christmas gift-giver at all. Other plans to reform Christmas advocated doing away with such Christmas figures entirely.

Christingle

The years after the Reformation were a time when priests and vicars experimented with different ways to best mark the birth of Christ in a manner befitting the man himself.

Many of these are now lost to time but one that still endures in the Church of England today is a service called the Christingle. The Christingle was developed in the eighteenth century by Johannes de Watteville, a pastor from a Protestant sect called the Moravian Church, and was intended as a way to capture the true meaning of Christmas. At Christmas services, de Watteville decided to hand the children in his congregation an inexpensive gift to symbolise the light of Christ. He chose an orange with a candle stuck in it.

The Christingle has developed a lot over recent years and was finally introduced to the UK by the Children's Society in 1968. At its heart was a simple ceremony to focus on the 'true meaning' of Christmas and abstain from the ostentation and artifice that surrounded the giving of gifts.

A story of the Christingle developed around three poor children who wanted to take an offering to church to honour Jesus but had no gift to give him. The only nice thing they owned was an orange, but even that had green skin on the top. Nonetheless, they decided to decorate the orange as best as they could – the eldest brother cut the skin off the top of the orange and put a candle into it to cover the gap. His sister decided to decorate the orange with a red ribbon and stick cocktail sticks into it and the youngest brother stuck some dried fruit on the cocktail sticks.

When they took this strange offering to church, the richer children all laughed at them for how pathetic their gift was and how much it paled in comparison to the gold, frankincense and myrrh that Jesus was offered by the Three Wise Men. However, when the priest saw it he was delighted that the children understood that the most important thing was to give what you could to Jesus and told them that they had understood the true meaning of Christmas.

At a Christingle service, children are all given an orange with a candle stuck on it and fruit and sweets stuck around the outside. The orange is said to represent the world, the red ribbon is the blood of Christ, the candle represents Christ himself and the dried fruit and sweets represent God's creations. Meanwhile, Christingle hymns are sung with titles such as 'Round Orange',

'It's Rounded Like an Orange' and 'Bring Your Christingle with Gladness and Joy'.

The War on Christmas

Odd though some of the new celebrations might have seemed, at least the Lutherans and Moravians wanted to keep Christmas, even if they were not so keen on some of the traditions that had developed around it. And why not? It was a popular celebration amongst the people, a boost of positivity against the horrors of winter and was a good focal point where everyone could come together and think about Jesus Christ.

However, some of the reformist groups within Protestantism were less tolerant – they not only believed St Nicholas and the Catholic trimmings of Christmas should be done away with. They wanted to get rid of Christmas altogether.

At first this seems a little bit strange – why would Christians want to get rid of one of their main days of celebration? For the answer to this you need to go back to the Gospels and the beginnings of Christianity.

To the early Christians, Christ's actual birth was not seen as a particularly big deal. In the New Testament, only Matthew and Luke actually talk about the nativity – and even then they disagree on several details. The gospels of Mark and John and the letters of Paul, which were all written earlier, don't bother to mention the circumstances of Christ's birth and the only focus on Christ was from his baptism onwards. To the early Christians it was the circumstances of Christ's death and resurrection – along with his teachings – that were important. When and how he had been born was an irrelevance – so much so that nobody even bothered to write a date of birth down.

In the early fourth century the Roman Emperor Constantine embraced and legalised Christianity. Christmas began to be celebrated on 25 December. It is not clear whether this was purely because it coincided with Saturnalia or whether early Christians genuinely believed Christ was born on 25 December, but certainly the Calvinist reformists (also known as the Puritans) a thousand years later felt that Christmas celebrations were an afterthought to the message of Christianity, and the date seemed to be a contrivance to fit in with pagan celebrations of winter. The Puritans wanted to purify Christianity and purge all the Catholic and pagan elements; to them, Christmas had no right to be in the Christian calendar.

If all that was not bad enough, the nature of the Christmas celebrations made everything much, much worse. Between the Lord of Misrule, the mumming and switches of social hierarchy that undermined religious authority, Christmas was a time of gambling, gluttony, drunkenness, debauchery, heathen rituals, dressing as the Devil, Papist celebrations and pagan remembrances. Everything the Puritans hated could be found in the celebration of Christmas.

In most of Europe Puritans existed but had limited influence. The Reformation had seen the Church split into several different factions and the moderate groups, closer to the traditions of the Catholic Church, tended to have the most power. Once they had got rid of their more extreme problems with the Catholic Church, they tended to let people get on with it as before. Which might have meant losing St Nicholas and all the Christmas characters that accompanied him, but at least Christmas itself was safe.

Not so in England, however.

One of the big problems in England was that the Reformation

169

was a bit of a token gesture. Whereas elsewhere in Europe people were reforming their churches in order to redistribute wealth, improve access to religion for the poor and to prevent people 'buying' religious salvation, in England the break from the Catholic Church really came in order for Henry VIII to put himself at the head of the English Church and be free to divorce his wife. The result of this was a break from the Catholic Church that was not really much of a reformation – most customs remained.

It was a compromise that angered both the Protestants – who wanted the new Church to be more of a break from the traditions of the Catholic Church – and the Catholics, who didn't want to break away at all. This led to a hundred years of squabbling and in-fighting as both the Catholics and Protestants took more and more extreme positions – people who would perhaps otherwise have been moderate reformers ended up being some of the most committed Puritans of all. This helped create the conditions for the English Civil War, the defeat and execution of King Charles I and the Puritan Oliver Cromwell seizing control of England and ultimately banning Christmas for sixteen years.

The banning of Christmas meant no public celebrations were allowed, no special religious services were permitted and shops had to be open as usual on Christmas Day. Puritan supporters would gather outside the houses of anyone who did celebrate Christmas to intimidate them into going to work, and would march around the street chanting anti-Christmas slogans.

The Puritans also strongly discouraged and intimidated anyone who did anything that suggested they *might* be supporting Christmas, even if it was not a clear public celebration. Eating mince pies, giving money to servants or sending gifts to friends in late December, and even putting sprigs of rosemary in roast

170

beef were seen as suspicious actions that could be met with threats and reprisals. In the countryside, there were even armed stand-offs between Puritans trying to close the churches and traditionalists trying to keep them open. The towns too had their problems. In Canterbury in 1647 the mayor might have forced shopkeepers to open their premises, but an angry mob smashing things in the shops very quickly ensured they were closed down again.

At the same time it is important to put this into perspective – not all Puritans supported the banning of Christmas. The ban was hard to enforce and the more moderate representatives of the Puritan authorities often turned a blind eye to celebrations, unless they were so public and obvious that they had to be seen to be doing something. Fines were far more often threatened than levied and, in many parts of the country, Christmas was banned in name only. Even religious Christmas services continued in private – it was generally only defiant attempts to publicly celebrate that resulted in arrests.

Certainly the ban brought an end to the drunken public Christmas celebrations that existed before the Reformation. Furthermore, the intimidation suffered by people who wanted to celebrate Christmas was deeply unpleasant. However, in England at least, Christmas was never under any severe threat of extinction.

Scotland

Scotland, however, was a different matter. Throughout medieval times, English and Scottish celebrations were mostly similar affairs, with widespread merriment (often fuelled by alcohol), singing, Lords of Misrule and festivals and rituals where the powerful and the not-so-powerful swapped places. However, in 1560 the Scottish Church formally broke with Catholicism and the Scottish Reformation began.

The new Calvinist Church of Scotland certainly tried to do a lot of good and its desire to build schools in every parish and to ensure improved relief to the poor was certainly laudable, but they were not big fans of Christmas. The Book of Discipline (which set out the rules and positions of the new Church) expressly forbade celebrations like Christmas and the Epiphany, and by the 1570s the Church was punishing people for such heinous acts as singing carols, making Yule-related bread and chanting the word Yule over and over at a New Year's Eve party.

Initially the ban was hard to enforce – the Scottish Church would regularly renew its criticisms and launch new crackdowns but found people just carried on as before. Even James VI, the King of Scotland, came under fire from the Church for celebrating Christmas. By 1640 the Church was searching people's houses for any signs of a goose (apparently a clear indication you were celebrating Christmas) or people taking the day off work. Almost a century of fighting for Christmas wore the population down and by 1650 the Church had largely succeeded in scuppering the celebrations. I say largely because, like the Alpine regions of Austria and Switzerland, many parts of the highlands and islands of Scotland are hard to access and the inhabitants found it quite easy to cannily circumvent any rules and regulations that did not suit them. The islands of the Outer Hebrides, for example, largely ignored the new rules and regulations and carried on celebrating Christmas much as before. But in the south the ban on Christmas was remarkably successful.

But how did the Church succeed in Scotland when it had

proved so difficult to ban Christmas everywhere else? The simple one-word answer was Hogmanay. People wanted a big midwinter celebration and the chance to act out their old traditions but actually it turned out that it did not have to be at Christmas. James VI moved New Years' Eve, which had until then been in the middle of March, to coincide with the end of December and, over the course of the seventeenth century, many of the old Christmas traditions became New Year traditions instead and, whilst the Church of Scotland continued to object for a while, eventually they accepted the compromise.

Hogmanay was tremendously successful – so much so that Scottish antipathy to Christmas celebrations lasted right the way into the middle of the twentieth century, and even now Hogmanay remains the most important celebration in many Scottish people's minds. This was not just a matter of religion. Scotland had become united with England (to many Scottish people's chagrin) and patriotism led many Scots to reject the Christmas that the English celebrated in favour of Scotland's unique celebration.

Scotland is not the only country with a traditional focus on the New Year rather than Christmas for political reasons. Russia, too, adopted a similar approach but in their case it was not the Protestant Reformation but the spread of Communism that led to their decision.

Russia

Describing early Christmas traditions across Russia is a bit difficult because, as any expert on the country will tell you, Russia is very big and so traditions varied from place to place. Church festivals were solemn but songs, costumes and trees were popular elsewhere. As an Orthodox country, these celebrations were not affected by the Reformation. However, there was one major difference to Central Europe – the role of St Nicholas.

As the patron saint of Russia, Nicholas had various other responsibilities there and it seemed that – perhaps save for a few small pockets in the west of the country that may have adopted customs they'd learned from others across Europe – he did not factor as a major gift-giver. Indeed, it is hard to find a tradition of gift-giving in Russia at all until the nineteenth century.

This was a time when Russia sought closer ties with Germany and when Russian high society took its lead from German fashions. This changed the nature of Christmas celebrations and led to the creation of a St Nicholas character. However, perhaps to avoid confusion with the Russian patron saint, he was called Ded Moroz or Grandfather Frost. Funnily enough, the character of Ded Moroz may have been a reinvention of a Slavic folktale featuring an evil wizard who froze children to death and carried them away in a sack. In the 19th Century he was reborn as a festive figure.

In 1914 Russia and Germany found themselves enemies in the Great War. Aping the Germans was strongly discouraged and suddenly Ded Moroz found himself deeply unpopular.

For a while after the war Christmas returned to normal (even though everything else was changing rapidly in the rest of Russian society) and Ded Moroz was restored. This did not last long, as the Soviet leaders hated Christmas as much as the Puritans did. As far as they were concerned, God was a myth, religion was an oppressive power structure and Christmas was a bourgeois celebration from a bygone age. In 1926 Stalin banned Christmas and, naturally, Ded Moroz went with him.

Like Cromwell and the Calvinists, Stalin learned a very important lesson. People really, really, like a midwinter celebration. Indeed, such celebrations predated Christianity and are perhaps an innate response to getting over the horrific winter conditions. Many people ignored the ban and many of those who obeyed it grew demoralised and unhappy. Over the next decade Stalin realised that cancelling Christmas had been a mistake that threatened to undermine his attempts to maintain his authority and his ability to keep control of his people. I don't know whether Stalin knew about the history of Christmas and Hogmanay in Scotland or not, but certainly he arrived at the exact same solution – move Christmas celebrations to New Year and remove the religious aspect. So Ded Moroz returned but now wholly disconnected from religion, and far from being St Nicholas, he was simply a bearded wizard. Neither the Catholics nor reformists would have liked that at all!

When Ded Moroz returned he was not alone – like any twentieth-century magician he brought with him a beautiful assistant. St Nicholas might have had gurning monsters with sticks and animal masks but the Russians were suffering enough from the realities of life under Communism. Instead, Ded Moroz had a beautiful and kind-hearted granddaughter (or sometimes niece) called Snegurouchka or the Snow Maiden.

Snegurouchka was actually a character from an existing folk story. The Snow Maiden was a princess carved out of ice who yearned and yearned to fall in love but found that her frozen heart prevented her from doing so. One day she finally got her wish, only to find that the love in her heart filled her with such warmth that she melted. Folktales are, of course, very different from fables and do not necessarily require a moral, but there is something about telling children a story where the moral seems to be 'love will kill you' that is brilliantly nihilistic.

In any case, the Snow Maiden was reborn. Since the fall of the Soviet Union, religious freedom has returned to Russia and

Christmas has started to make a tentative comeback, but New Year remains the main celebration and Santa Claus is yet to usurp Ded Moroz and Snegurouchka in the affections of Russian children.

Babushka

Speaking of Russian folktales, it is impossible to go through a book on Christmas tales without talking about the story of Babushka.

Babushka was an elderly Russian lady who lived alone in a forest. She spent her days cooking, cleaning and chopping wood, but she was elderly and her household chores took her a long time. One day she heard a knock on the door and encountered three wise men who were seeking shelter. She invited them in and, over a delicious but laboriously prepared meal, they told her that they were following a star to witness the birth of a king. Babushka expressed a wish to join them and they invited her to come along. However, the elderly lady sighed and wistfully said that, much as she would love to do so, she would need to finish cleaning and preparing her house first.

Babushka promised that once she had finished she would follow on, find the star and catch them up. She struggled and laboured and a few days later she finished cleaning her house and set out after them, carrying a bag of home-made sweets and gifts for the newborn baby. However, the star could not be seen, the wise men were long gone, and she never did catch them up. She is now said to wander Russia (and latterly the world) handing out presents to children she encounters in the hope that they might be the baby she seeks.

To many people in America and the UK, Babushka is perhaps

the most famous Russian folktale of all. It is a popular Christmas play for schoolchildren and, in my own school, used to form part of Christingle services. When I have talked about this book to friends, Babushka is the character I have been asked about the most.

However, there is one small problem. Despite her status as a famous Russian folk character, it is surprisingly hard to find evidence that Babushka existed in Russian folklore at all. This is hard to be certain of – obviously Russia has a huge amount of mythology in different regions and it is difficult to become acquainted with every variant or story that has been told – but certainly when Alexander Afanasyev, the Russian equivalent of the Brothers Grimm, collected and published 600 Russian folktales in 1855,[28] Babushka seems to be conspicuous by her absence.

So where does Babushka come from? Australian/Russian writer Irene Woodhead traces the origin of the story to a 1907 book of poetry written by Edith Mathilda Thomas, which was published in America, and suggests that the myth spread from there. Thomas presents the story as a Russian folktale but her source is not entirely clear.

What is striking is that the central figure of the story is actually almost exactly the same as the Italian character of La Befana, a traditional gift-giver in Italy who delivers presents the night before Epiphany. La Befana is considerably nicer than most of her gift-bringing counterparts of days gone by. It might be true that she would leave coal for naughty children but, being a good housekeeper, she would also use a broom to sweep the floor clean and – in doing so – sweep away the problems of the year. The fact she was an old woman may have been intended to represent the old year which had just passed and which needed to pass its mantle on to the new year.

The Rise of a Familiar Figure

The rise of Protestantism saw Europe divided into Catholic and Protestant regions. In Catholic areas such as Italy, most of France and southern Germany, Austria and much of southern Europe, St Nicholas continued to visit as before, although his pagan assistants began to be phased out. In Protestant areas – much of northern Germany, parts of eastern Europe and the Lowlands – St Nicholas was replaced by new figures such as the Christ Child. Finland, Iceland and Scandinavia also came under Protestant influence and traditions such as the Yule Lads, Joulupukki and the tomte were strongly discouraged and, for some periods, banned. St Nicholas was even briefly banned in the Netherlands, the country where he is most popular today!

Puritan bans on Christmas ultimately did not succeed. The English ban on Christmas lasted just sixteen years and even Scotland is now celebrating Christmas again. True, some of the heathen customs and drunken debauchery of yesteryear have now disappeared, but ultimately Christmas returned to England in a stronger form than ever before. The Puritans had more success in America. In New England Christmas celebrations were banned during the seventeenth century and Christmas did not become a popular festival until the late nineteenth century.

One of the major reasons why the banning of Christmas failed in England was because the threat of abolition caused people in the seventeenth century to fight for their right to continue the traditions they had developed. Many writers even tried to find a character who embodied these Christmas traditions and could be used to guarantee their safekeeping. Writers of the seventeenth century were not masters of subtlety – probably because large segments of the public were illiterate. So books had a limited reach,

178

and playwrights knew that drunken audiences would talk and heckle through most of their plays, and thus needed constant reminders of what was going on. Ben Jonson's 1616 play *Christmas, His Masque* features a group of allegorical brothers and sisters with names like Minced Pie, Carol, Mumming, Wassail and Misrule, and he then introduces their father. The father is an old man with a beard who bemoans the fact that he is being excluded from Christmas celebrations and implores the audience to keep the traditions alive in the face of growing opposition.

This is an early appearance of a character who would soon be featuring in mummers' plays, stories and newspaper articles everywhere, and who over the next few hundred years would come to be a ubiquitous figure. He was a character who came to embody the secular, irreligious Christmas traditions that the Puritans despised, but perhaps it was only because of the Puritan's opposition that he ever developed at all. His name, as you might have guessed, was Father Christmas.

Reinventing Christmas

*The Christmas Man (England,
Germany and France)*

The Puritan attempts to ban Christmas may have ultimately failed, but they fundamentally changed how Christmas was celebrated. For a century or two, Christmas was a wounded animal, slinking in the shadows and licking its wounds. Celebrations were small, private affairs with perhaps a special meal and a quiet church service. Newspapers and diaries that survive from the time tend to give it a mere passing mention. It was not until the nineteenth century that it would return to the limelight and, when it did, a metamorphosis had happened and it was a completely new beast that emerged.

King Charles II may have been restored to the throne of England and the influence of the Puritans may have been tempered, but Christmas was not what it used to be. Many of the boisterous activities of the medieval Christmases never returned. The masked marauders of mummery were confined to plays and pageants, whilst the Lord of Misrule and Feast of Fools were largely abolished. The Bean King and Pea Queen celebrations on 6 January did briefly re-emerge but were ultimately curtailed by the Industrial Revolution. Twelve-day Christmas holidays were lost and the Epiphany celebrations were consumed by the demands that the captains of industry placed on their workforce. By the time the Bank Holiday Act came into force in 1871, only Christmas Day and Boxing Day were included. Christmas had got shorter and – aside from the Twelfth Cake, which was re-branded as Christmas cake – few of the traditions of Epiphany survived. Epiphany celebrations survived in Spain and parts of

France and Portugal, but much of Europe simply came to treat 6 January as just another day.

Most importantly of all, Christmas seemed to have ceased to matter. Celebrations were minimal and private. Shops stayed open and it was largely business as usual. In a 45-year period from 1790 to 1835, more than a century after Christmas had been saved from the Puritan suppression, December issues of *The Times* newspaper only briefly mentioned Christmas in twenty-five of those years and did not mention it at all in the other twenty.[29] Christmas was a relic of the past when agricultural communities held midwinter festivals to celebrate the completion of the harvest and to quell fear and boredom during the seemingly endless wait for the sun to return. What place could it possibly have in an industrial world where those communities were divided into cities and where work continued right through the winter? Christmas might not have been dead but the celebrations seemed irrelevant.

A Christmas Miracle

Yet by the end of the nineteenth century Christmas was back and was bigger and more popular than ever. It was like a Christmas miracle – perhaps the most literal one of all.

Gradually, as the initial intensity of the Puritans, Pietists and Calvinists began to fade and religious tolerance increased, people began to revive the festive season. England was the dominant global superpower of the nineteenth century and so was in the strongest position to influence traditions and customs across Europe. As the century progressed this global power base gradually began to shift towards America. Both countries played a large part in the Christmas revival. Christmas had not dwindled in some parts of Europe in quite as extreme a way as it had in England, but the celebrations in many countries had grown stagnant, neutered by religious objections and half-forgotten due to the changes of the Industrial Age. St Nicholas was banned in many areas and his assistants had died out in most of Europe.

The Victorians – most famously Prince Albert and Queen Victoria – embraced the festive season and revived or adopted countless traditions. Christmas cards, Christmas presents, Christmas trees (in England) and modern Christmas decorations like tinsel and baubles all stem from the second half of the nineteenth century. So too does a jolly man with a beard called Father Christmas delivering presents to children. It is scarcely exaggeration to say that the Victorians – and their counterparts across Europe – invented the modern Christmas.

However, invention was not actually the Victorians' intention. All that the supporters of Christmas were doing was trying to capture the Christmas of days gone by. Like so many people today, the Victorians yearned for that mythical Christmas of yesteryear. But why the sudden resurrection of a festival that seemed to be dying out just decades earlier?

The simple answer may have been colonialism. Although there were European settlements in America from the seventeenth century onwards, it was only in the eighteenth and nineteenth centuries that global expansion happened in earnest and countries really raced to conquer and settle in every territory of the world. At first this was merely about expansion, subjugation and commercial exploitation. However, after the campaign to abolish the slave trade in the early nineteenth century, the thrust of colonialism changed. Whereas early colonists were happy to abuse and destroy supposedly inferior races in the name of economic gains for the Motherland, countries like Britain began to seek a moral purpose to justify conquering and dominating their territories.

As Jeremy Paxman puts it in his book on the British Empire: '... the entire imperial purpose was a vocation to civilise the world, an enterprise in salvation. It rested on a conviction not merely that different races had different characteristics but that the qualities of the British were superior to all others.'[30]

Nowadays the notion seems preposterous and, even at the time, it was really about morally justifying the abuses inflicted on indigenous populations rather than eradicating them, but even though it did not improve life for the occupied and oppressed, it caused a huge shift in how the Europeans viewed themselves and their countries' history. The same non-Christian elements of traditions and folklore that had been denounced as pagan two centuries earlier now became proof of the unique nature of a country's cultural history and national qualities. All of a sudden, folk stories and pagan ritual became evidence of an imperial nation's right to rule.

All across Europe nationalist movements sprang up. In Germany the Brothers Grimm collected folktales and shared them as evidence of the German identity. Britain created John Bull as an image of 'Britishness' and devised a set of 'British' values around fair play, honesty and bravery, which were taught to aspiring colonists via the public school system. In Denmark, Norway and Sweden Scandinavianists such as Hans Christian Andersen worked to cultivate a Scandinavian identity. And in the search for these unique national qualities, people looked to the past to try to discover the 'essence' of their nation.

In England, certainly, it is hard to separate the revival of Christmas from the Victorian perception of Britishness (which really meant Englishness – the Scots and Welsh were largely

185

expected to assimilate or be ignored). Swiftly, the almost-forgotten traditions of Christmas became central to English identity. As a religious festival Christmas had a moral and ethical kudos that fitted in well with promoting traditional Christian values.

Christmas became the ultimate expression of Englishness and – if you found yourself elsewhere in the Empire – the ultimate reminder of home. In 1873 the *Christmas Story-teller* summed up the importance of Christmas to the British identity in words which almost certainly work best if you imagine them in the voice of Hugh Laurie playing Bertie Wooster:

> Where is the Englishman to be found who has not felt that he has lost a chapter out of life's duodecimo if he passed a Christmas day without in some sort distinguishing it from the other three hundred and sixty-four days? Whether in the arctic regions of the torrid zone, or away in the southern seas amongst the whalers, or wandering on the western prairies, the Englishman remembers the familiar words 'Merry Christmas and a happy New Year'.[31]

What's more, the need for midwinter celebrations was as strong as ever. As people moved from the countryside to the cities to find work, or even migrated overseas to the colonies, the depressing, long winter nights made them nostalgic for home – perhaps even more so, ironically, when people were in countries where those long winter nights were only noticeable by their absence! Somehow, in the heat of a burning sun, the image of snow-lined streets and roaring log fires took on a poignancy and nostalgia (even today Australian Christmas cards frequently depict winter scenes, despite Christmas happening at the height of summer).

Christmas traditions became less of a tool for surviving harsh winters and more of a reminder of home, and the traditional Christmas of yesteryear became a nostalgic symbol of all that British colonialists were fighting for and all that they were leaving behind. Christmas became a time for looking to the past and, without realising it, the Victorians embarked on a conquest to capture a mythical perfect Christmas of the past. It is a quest many of us still pursue to this day.

There were two problems with this. Firstly, nobody could actually remember what this fantastic Christmas of the past used to look like. Secondly, if they could, they probably would not really have liked the results.

Society had changed a lot in the 200 years that Christmas had become marginalised. From Roman times to the Middle Ages, midwinter celebrations had mostly been about agricultural communities letting off steam during the barren winter months through rowdy partying, celebrating the fact there was little work to do now that the harvest was over and alleviating their fears of the dangers of winter.

Now things were different. Puritanism was gone but rowdy partying was largely discouraged, especially amongst the newly formed middle classes who were anxious not to demean their new-found social status; the Industrial Revolution had meant employment switched from farms to factories where work no longer stopped for the winter; and – though the housing situation in cities was far from perfect – it was filth and overcrowding, rather than the dangers of the weather, that tended to cause more danger to the Victorian population. Christmas had to find a new meaning.

Ultimately that new meaning came from two things – first of all, the emphasis on a family celebration where the heart of Christmas was a focus on children and the innocent wonder of the magic of the season. And secondly, the idea of the Christmas spirit of charity, togetherness and goodwill to all men.

Charity at Christmas was not a new concept, of course. The Church had been giving to the poor on St Nicholas's Day since medieval times, and the era of mumming had seen landlords – terrified of being roughed up by wassailing peasants – handing out gifts. But charity and goodwill was certainly not foremost in the minds of the youths nailing strangers to shop doors or of the priests who supposedly threw dung at their congregation during the Feast of Fools. Besides, in the feudal societies of the past, nearly everyone was a peasant struggling to survive and giving most of their produce to their lords. Most people were therefore in need of charity rather than in a position to hand it out!

But now the Industrial Revolution had created a middle class who were able to give money to charity. In fact they were able to spend money in general and very willing to do so to prove their status. They demanded a more sedate Christmas befitting of their 'superior' position, removed from the drunken antics of the ruffians of the lower orders. That usually meant spending Christmas at home and treating the family. Christmas decorations – which had consisted of holly, ivy and other greenery in medieval times and had dwindled since the Civil War – were revived and grew more elaborate as people were willing to spend money buying decorations fashioned by craftsmen or produced in factories. The Industrial Revolution might have meant people were scattered across the country and distant from their friends and relatives, but the new postal service created an opportunity for people to send shop-bought postcards and Christmas cards around the country. And Christmas presents – previously small, inexpensive tokens and novelty items, where they even existed before – began to become more expensive.

Whereas once children got only fruit or sweets, now toys and gifts began to appear. Adults began exchanging gifts too. And who was to deliver those gifts? St Nicholas and his companions from days gone by? The Christkind or the invented figures of the Puritans? The Victorians – and their Christmas revivalist counterparts across Europe and America – did not merely capture the past. A host of new Christmas-givers were created and presented as though they had been around forever. For a while, these characters competed for domination, each having their sphere of influence but none of them managing to dominate outright. Then, ultimately, a candidate emerged in New York who was to become the most famous gift-giver in history.

A Cavalcade of Gift-Bringers

The newly invented figures did not mean that it was all over for our creepy Christmas characters. St Nicholas, as we know, survived and still delivers presents in the Netherlands and parts of Germany and Central Europe to this day. The Three Kings emerged in Spain. Perchta, Knecht Ruprecht, Zwarte Piet and Schmutzli all re-emerged from hiding to publicly accompany St Nicholas and other Santa figures around Europe.

But something had changed. Many of these characters were pale shadows of what had gone before. Sometimes they adopted the Christ Child's example and only visited during the nighttime, thus meaning the costumed characters were seen no more. Where they did appear during the day, they were not quite as menacing as before. They still ranted and raved at naughty children and made threats to punish them, but now parents treated those threats as a joke – a game that was a relic of a bygone era. The children were not as scared as they had been before because

189

they knew the bark of these characters was worse than their bite. Fortunately, the Krampus was as terrifying as ever and really came into his own in the age of the Christmas card, but many of his counterparts began to go soft.

Increasingly, Santa's evil assistants became mere figures of fun. I wrote before about how Zwarte Piet went from the Devil to a racial caricature with black skin, bright red lips, shiny jewellery and a 'comedy' accent. This not only made the character considerably more offensive to later generations, it made him far less frightening too. In a contest between an enslaved devil, chained up and dragged in from Hell to beat you, toss you into a sack and drag you to eternal damnation, and a minstrel with a ropey accent, it is quite clear which is the more terrifying.

By now St Nicholas was starting to mellow into a nicer character. Just as with his demonic assistants, the threats of eternal damnation began to fade and a kinder, more child-friendly Nicholas began to emerge. The threats of whippings and being spirited into a sack still remained, but they were not made with the same intensity and plausibility of medieval times – and many children were already beaten too often for another beating to be a truly terrifying prospect.

Christmas Man (Germany)

The areas of Europe that had remained Catholic still saw St Nicholas as the archetypical gift-bringer, and children continued to welcome his visit in those areas. It seems that many Protestants wanted him back too. However, there was still a fundamental problem – St Nicholas was a saint and the Protestants were not supposed to honour saints. Instead, during the course of the eighteenth century, Protestants invented their own Christmas figures.

In Germany this was the Weinnachtsmann or, to give the English translation, Christmas Man.

The Christmas Man's name was fantastically literal; he was a man who gave gifts at Christmas. As it turned out he was a bearded old man, much like St Nicholas. He called on houses to hand out presents to children who had behaved, much like St Nicholas. And he carried a birch rod to beat naughty children, much like St Nicholas.

However, the crucial thing for the Protestants was that he was most definitely *not* St Nicholas. In fact, he was most definitely not a saint at all. In order to definitely not be a saint, he definitely did not wear bishop's robes or any other religious insignia. And he certainly did not deliver presents on St Nicholas's Day. Like the Christkind, he instead delivered them on Christmas Day. Which definitely made him the Christmas Man. Definitely, definitely, *definitely* not St Nicholas. Nope. All similarities to St Nicholas were entirely coincidental. Definitely.

The Christmas Man was very popular in Germany and soon he was joined by other Protestant Christmas Men across Europe. The French – who had busily been separating Church and State and did not want a saint either – created their own character of Père Noël. He was sometimes joined by our good old friend Père Fouettard, just in case naughty children needed to be punished. The English, who had never actually had St Nicholas in the first place, embraced this new tradition and rewarded their old saviour of Christmas – Father Christmas himself – with a promotion. Elsewhere, Old Man Winter and Father Frost carried out a similar role. What's more, these secular characters of no fixed religion helped set the scene for the most famous gift-giver of all to emerge and transcend religions as he conquered the world. We'll come to him soon.

Christmas Man was not the only Protestant gift-bringer. They also had the Christkind, that wonderful Lutheran creation of a floating baby Jesus who somehow managed to deliver Christmas presents twenty-four hours before actually being born. By now, it had become clear that this character was never going to be a hit with children, but ultimately parents found a way to reinvent the character so it had more appeal. Instead of being a baby, the Christkind became a small child – usually a girl – dressed all in white with a jewelled crown and gold wings. The Christkind had effectively gone from Jesus to angel.

This transformation made a lot of sense. Angels were already a traditional part of Christmas. In the nativity, it is the archangel Gabriel who tells an elderly couple they will have a son (who will be John the Baptist) and tells Mary that she will give birth to Jesus, and an angel that reassures Joseph that his wife's scarcely plausible explanation of her pregnancy actually holds together. Angels also appear after the birth to tell the shepherds of the divine gift and to sing of Jesus's glory. Angels were also a major feature of pageants and Christmas parades. Parents would dress their children – especially girls – up as angels in the festive season. Therefore a Christmas gift-bringer who looked like a child dressed as an angel was popular both with parents, who could imagine their angelic son or daughter in that role, and also with children, who could aspire to be an angel themselves.

Angels were not the only supernatural creatures to achieve popularity in the nineteenth-century Christmas. Fairies were very popular too. The fairies of Victorian times, however, were markedly different from the faeries I've talked about in Scotland, Ireland, Scandinavia and the Shetland Isles. Faeries were malevolent supernatural beings who would steal children, spirit away husbands or wives, or play wicked tricks on the human population. Fairies were much more like we imagine them today. Victorians loved the image of tiny magical human-like creatures with wings, living amongst the undergrowth and ostensibly acting out human lives on a much smaller scale. Artists would depict them enjoying 'fairy' Christmases with miniature decorations and rats or voles for meat.

Postcards of Christmas Men

Images and illustrations became far more widely available during the nineteenth century than they had ever been before. It was the century when cheap mass-produced Christmas cards and postcards became available so, for the first time, images of Christmas gift-bringers were not confined to the depths of the imagination or what your neighbour could achieve from his dressing-up box. Instead the Victorians had professional paintings, some of which survive to this day and give us clear pictorial evidence of what Victorians thought these characters looked like.

Postcards of the Christkind or other angelic gift-bringers would often show winged children or young women riding horse-drawn sleds across the snow. An 1880s postcard of the Christkind shows her to be an adult-sized child handing out presents to children of a similar age. Angels could wear pink or blue but usually wore white, had wings, a halo and sometimes carried a harp. They look a lot like the angels of today. Postcards of fairies look very much as you might imagine – tiny winged creatures in the forests dancing across streams, sitting on toadstools eating Christmas feasts or teasing and tormenting animals. It was a very pleasant, albeit rather twee, Christmas scene.

Other Christmas cards are a little stranger and harder to fathom. The strangest without question are the Christmas cards of dead birds – a picture of a fully formed robin or wren lying on its back, presumably having died from the cold, with the words 'May Yours Be a Joyful Christmas' or 'A Loving Christmas Greeting' written on the back. John Grossman, who chronicles Christmas cards in his wonderful book *Christmas Curiosities*, guesses that it might have been a combination of eliciting sympathy and sentimental feelings from the receiver and a stark reminder of those less fortunate at Christmastime, but frankly a dead bird remains a bizarre thing to put on a postcard. It should be noted that living animals were popular too. They were often anthropomorphised and carrying out human Christmas activities. A robin giving to the poor, rodents drinking in their local pub, a cat dressed as a ballerina and pre-paring to perform – the usual sort of thing! Pantomime clowns were also very popular. So too, depressingly, were caricatures of black-faced minstrels.

And what of Father Christmas, Père Noël and the other Pro-testant Christmas Men? Generally, they were simply depicted as elderly men in furs or winter coats. It is hard to tell how much of this image was influenced by events in the USA as postcards did not exist until the 1860s, by which time Santa Claus had been invented and may have already been an influence. Certainly the earliest postcards show a man with a white beard, but generally the overall look screamed 'ageing tramp or beggar' rather than wonderful magical elf. He was scruffy, his clothes were ragged and, far from smiling, he often looked tired or forlorn.

A great number of the earliest postcards of the Weinnacht-smann and Père Noël still focused on their tendency to punish children. They would often be pictured sitting with a child laid across their knee and a stick or branch in their raised arm. The most dramatic Weinnachtsmann postcard shows him tying a child to the branch of a tree, so that he had both arms free to administer a beating. This is not a man who would pass a CRB check.

Father Christmas tended to be a little more wild and rural-looking than his European counterparts. His history as a traditional Christmas figure representing the 'pagan' Christmases of yore still stood strong and he would frequently be captured with a crown of holly on his head, branches in his hand and occasionally even wearing items of shrubbery! Generally, he too was a gentrified figure, depicted at civilised middle-class houses and appearing rather sober.

The transport of these early characters varied a great deal. From an early stage, Father Christmas and the Protestant Christmas men were sometimes pictured on a sled. However, the sled was pulled by horses rather than reindeer. What's more, a sled was just one of a variety of methods of transport which the old men of Christmas might use. White horses and boats were both used too, betraying how closely the Christmas Men resembled Sinterklaas. However, he was a man of the modern age and could sometimes be portrayed riding on a new-fangled contraption like a steam train or a bicycle.

Even at this early stage, characters were already recognisable relations to their cousin from across the Atlantic, and whilst it is true that, over the next hundred years, their identity would gradually be subsumed into his, it was certainly not a massive cultural leap or change of identity in the way that would happen with the tomte, Joulupukki or the Yule Lads, who were already being depicted in red occasionally.

The Mystery of Diedrich Knickerbocker

With Christmas visitors becoming more benign, and the popularity of the Christmas Men finally shaking the image of St Nicholas free from its main obstacles to popularity outside of the Catholic population, the stage was finally set for the most famous figure of all to make his entrance. The story of Santa Claus starts, as every good story should, with the link between a missing historian, a famous dessert, a pair of women's knickers and the New York professional basketball team.

Prior to the time of the missing historian in question, Christmas had enjoyed a chequered history in America. When the first Europeans fled there to escape religious persecution, many brought with them the traditions of misrule and chaos that had shaped the Christmas of the Middle Ages. The southern states had carried on celebrations much as their ancestors had before the Reformation, with drinking, feasting, dancing, wild partying and – this being America – gunfire. As in England, masked working-class revellers would wander from house to house demanding food and drink and threatening destruction.

In the North, colonies such as New England were founded by Puritans, so Christmas was largely opposed – and even banned outright – well into the nineteenth century. Although America's foundation was hugely influenced by religious exiles fleeing persecution, it was not always the same religious exiles or beliefs. This was not too much of a problem at first – colonies were set up by people with shared beliefs and attitudes, and America was too vast and sparsely populated for the different factions to need to mingle together. Tensions increased as American cities expanded in the wake of the Industrial Revolution. By the beginning of the nineteenth century there were particular difficulties in the cities of the northeast, such as Boston, Philadelphia and New York.

The essential problem was a class divide. Working-class revellers would roam the streets at Christmas forming calithump bands – impromptu and tuneless orchestras of drunks with horns, whistles and pots and pans – making as much noise as possible. Mumming was popular and even today Philadelphia still celebrates New Year's Day with a Mummers' Parade. They would visit middle-class houses and put on bawdy shows with lewd jokes, before demanding hospitality and gifts in return. The middle classes wanted peace and relaxation with their families. They did not welcome visits from drunken oiks swearing, drinking and putting on vulgar shows, especially when this unpleasantness was compounded by being asked to hand out gifts and food to the very people who were pestering them.

What's more, drunken Christmas riots were a frequent occurrence. Perhaps the most vivid example was in 1826 when cadets at the US Military Academy in New York were banned from drinking at Christmas. A few decided to do so anyway but slipped a bit too much whisky in their eggnog. What began with nine cadets having a quiet drink on Christmas Eve ended up with a lieutenant knocked unconscious and one third of the cadets taking up arms against their superiors in the mistaken belief that they were about to be assaulted by the full might of the US Army.

Such bacchanalia was not for everyone. In the nineteenth century police began to crack down on the anarchic, drunken rowdiness, and newspapers like the *New York Herald* urged their readers to 'avoid taverns and grog shops, for a few days at least, and spend their money at home'.[32] Meanwhile, churches campaigned for Christmas to be made a legal holiday in order to encourage families and their servants to stay at home and not venture into town.

Some conservative social thinkers and writers took a more practical approach and actively tried to reshape Christmas traditions into something more socially acceptable and popular with middle-class families. They realised that the drunken Christmas celebrations would only dissipate if they put something in their place. But what to replace them with?

The answer came after the disappearance of the New York amateur historian Diedrich Knickerbocker. Diedrich Knickerbocker was of Dutch ancestry and his major historical research project *A History of New York*, which was published in 1809, told the story of the early Dutch settlers to what was then New Amsterdam. Knickerbocker himself had disappeared by the time of publication. He had been staying in the Columbian Hotel in New York but had disappeared without paying. The manuscript of the book was found amongst his belongings and the landlord, keen to recoup his lost rent, decided to publish the book. Adverts were placed in the local newspapers trying to find Diedrich Knickerbocker, but the mystery of his disappearance remained unsolved for many months. Even after the truth was discovered, Diedrich Knickerbocker was never seen again. To this day, his body has never been found.

Nonetheless, Knickerbocker's research is significant, as it shows the point where St Nicholas became Santa. He describes the Christmas traditions of the first Dutch settlers, the building of the Church of St Nicholas (the first church ever built in New York) and the place that St Nicholas's Day held in the hearts of early New Yorkers. He explains how St Nicholas flew over the houses in a cart pulled by horses and how he would shimmy down chimneys to deliver gifts. Essentially, the description was so vivid that Knickerbocker became the first man to chronicle the modern Santa Claus.

There were two very small problems with all of this. The first is that Diedrich Knickerbocker never actually existed. The second is that the 'traditional celebrations' he described were entirely fictional. *A History of New York* was a practical joke. Two hundred years later, with Santa Claus one of the most recognisable figures in the world, it is fair to say that it's a joke that has got way out of hand.

In actual fact, Knickerbocker's *History of New York* was an elaborate joke by the then-unknown writer Washington Irving, who would later become famous as the writer of 'Rip Van Winkle' and 'The Legend of Sleepy Hollow'. Then in his mid-twenties, Irving had made his writing debut a few years earlier when a series of letters were published in the *New York Chronicle* under the pseudonym Jonathan Oldstyle, letters which were designed to goad two rival local theatre critics into a public slanging match. Once the two critics, several actors and a theatre director were tearing each other's throats out, Oldstyle, with the grace and mock-innocence of the best modern-day internet troll, wrote a further letter expressing bafflement as to how he'd inadvertently provoked such a reaction.

Knickerbocker's *History of New York* was written in reaction to Samuel Latham Mitchill's *The Picture of New York*, which Irving had found dull and pretentious. It was intended as a satire of stolid, worthy and pompous history books, and the debacle around Dietrich Knickerbocker was partly a joke and partly a publicity stunt that had several unexpected consequences.

Firstly, Diedrich Knickerbocker himself, for a man who never existed, turned out to be distinctly influential. The word Knickerbocker became a slang term for New Yorkers with Dutch ancestry and ultimately, New York itself. The New York Knicks and the Knickerbocker Glory ice cream sundae both take their name from the fictional character. When the book was published in England, the illustrations were done by Charles Dickens's illustrator – a man named George Cruikshank. Cruikshank's drawings of old-style Dutch trousers resembled ladies undergarments of the day and ultimately led to female underwear being referred to as 'knickers'. I have a sneaking suspicion that you were not expecting this particular fact in a book about Christmas ...

Secondly, whilst Irving's traditions of St Nicholas in New York were almost certainly invented by him on the spot, they turned out to be surprisingly popular. St Nicholas might not have been known to fly through the skies and climb down chimneys before Irving's writings, but he quickly gained a reputation for it. The following year John Pintard published a pamphlet extolling the virtues of traditional Sinterklaas celebrations.

Pintard, like Irving, was a member of the New York Historical Society. Although a Protestant, he believed – perhaps rather patronisingly – that the absence of Sinterklaas and the pagan rituals that used to exist in Europe denied the working classes an organised and safe way to celebrate Christmas, and thus led to chaos and anarchy. It is very possible that Pintard's enthusiasm for Sinterklaas celebrations were how Irving learned about St Nicholas.

Two weeks after Pintard's pamphlet was published an anonymous poem in a New York newspaper praised 'Sancte Claus' for his gift-giving. The popularity seems to have snowballed from there, for in 1812, three years after Irving's publication, one Samuel Woods was trying to debunk the children's myth of 'Old Santa Claw'. It was starting to become clear that Washington Irving's practical joke had kick-started a phenomenon.

But when and where had Sinterklaas become Santa Claus? The exact point is difficult to determine but the name became popular as an alternative name for St Nicholas's Eve before the saint had been resurrected as a Christmas character. On 26 December 1773 the *New York Gazette* referred to 'St. Nicholas, also called St. A Claus'. On 25 January 1808 the satirical periodical *Salmagundi* referred to St Nicholas as being 'vulgarly called Santaclaus', although the fact that said periodical was written by none other than Washington Irving makes it hard to be sure of the veracity of the claim!

Washington Irving's influence on the American Christmas does not end there. In 1819 and 1820, whilst living in England, he published *The Sketch Book*, which included a series of stories set in a fictional country house named Bracebridge Hall that popularised English Christmas traditions of the past in America (and indeed in England too). Along with Charles Dickens, Irving's writings did more than anyone to promote the idyllic traditional Christmas and set out the customs and traditions that form part of our ideal Christmas today. Much like Dickens's Christmas stories, Washington Irving's tales purported to capture the spirit of Christmas traditions of yesteryear but actually helped invent much of what we now think of as the 'traditional' Christmas. Although Irving had spent a lot of time at Aston Hall near Birmingham, he later admitted he never actually witnessed any of the Christmas traditions that he described.

Clement Clarke Moore versus Henry Livingston

Santa would have got nowhere had nobody carried on Irving's work, and it was an anonymous poem published in the New York *Sentinel* in 1822 that really invented Santa Claus in the public consciousness. It did not actually mention Santa by name, but 'A Visit from St Nicholas' – much better known as 'The Night Before Christmas' – nonetheless was the source of many of our modern ideas about Santa. Reindeer are introduced for the first time too – eight of them, in fact, complete with their names. The ninth reindeer – Rudolph – would be added over a hundred years later. The sudden introduction of this animal is strange and surprising – especially as, up until this point and even within 'The Night Before Christmas', there is nothing to associate St Nicholas or Santa Claus with the North Pole.[33]

The St Nicholas of the poem, despite his name, had lost his holiness. Like Father Christmas, the Weinnachtsmann or one of the Protestant Christmas figures, he has no mitre or staff, wears fur instead of a bishop's robes and he even comes on Christmas Eve rather than St Nicholas's Day. He is presented as a merry figure with a pipe, a round belly and a jolly laugh, a world away from the austere St Nicholas with his threats of violence and punishment. However, unlike those Christmas Men there is a supernatural element too – not only does the sleigh fly but he is described as a tiny elf, so small that he can easily 'bound' down the chimney. This chimney-hopping is a detail that remained even after later illustrations restored him to full size. Although the European Christmas Men were obviously Protestant adaptations of St Nicholas, Irving's book and the 1822 poem are the first occasions where St Nicholas himself is presented as a secular figure.

The other striking similarity between Knickerbocker's *History of New York* and 'A Visit from St Nicholas' is that there was a dispute over the authorship. The poem was originally published anonymously but fifteen years later was credited to Clement Clarke Moore. Moore had not originally claimed authorship because he was keen to present himself as a 'serious' writer of academic works. The poem had been sent to the *Sentinel* without his knowledge and he only included it amongst his own works once his children urged him to do so.

Some years later, the family of a man named Major Henry Livingstone Jr claimed that the reason Moore had never previously taken the credit was because their now-deceased relative, rather than Moore, was the real author.

Livingstone himself lived for seven years after the poem was published and had never actually claimed authorship of the poem either. However, members of his family claimed to remember him reading it fifteen years before publication, and – interestingly – two years before Washington Irving had gone to print. The Livingstone family have never been able to provide any conclusive evidence to back up the claims for their ancestor though, whereas numerous people close to Moore, including the person who submitted it for publication, confidently attested that he was the author. It is likely that the dispute over the authorship will never be resolved conclusively, but Clement Clarke Moore is widely credited with the poem, and his claim seems the more plausible one.

If Moore did write the poem, where did he get the ideas from? He may have been influenced by a little-known poem, also anonymous, published in 1821 in a series of children's books called *The Children's Friend* by William Gilley, an acquaintance of Moore. This poem is much less well known than 'A Visit from

St Nicholas' but does refer to St Nicholas as 'Old Santeclaus' and, like Moore's poem, features a reindeer-pulled sleigh, albeit with just the one reindeer and an inability to fly.

This aside, however, the poem is much closer to Sinterklaas than Santa Claus. The illustrations show a full-sized slim adult bishop and he only delivers presents to 'good' children. Like St Nicholas and his European antecedents, he leaves naughty children sticks so their parents can beat them. Even the presents are books to promote knowledge – noisy or mischief-making toys are strictly off limits. Clement Clarke Moore's poem, which presented a happy elf flying on a sleigh pulled by eight reindeer, seemingly unperturbed by how well or badly children had behaved, was a far bigger revolution.

Moore may have got many more ideas from the same place as Washington Irving. Although Moore was not of Dutch origin, he was a member of the New York Historical Society – alongside John Pintard and Washington Irving – and would have learned about the Dutch St Nicholas traditions from there. The Dutch settlers who founded New York were Protestants and, despite having knowledge of St Nicholas from Dutch history, would not have venerated saints. Essentially, what Irving and Moore did, perhaps without intending to, was to present the character without the religious convictions and historical baggage that had shaped the character of St Nicholas and his European associates.

Santa Claus Comes to Town

Heavily influenced by European folklore, but created by Americans who were far enough removed from that folklore to reinvent it as they saw fit, Santa Claus was free to develop in any way writers and storytellers chose to present him. St Nicholas was bound to the ideology of medieval Christianity, where poor biblical knowledge or sinful behaviour meant eternal damnation. Meanwhile, the likes of the Krampus and Schmutzli were tied to the cold, harsh, rural winters where strange creatures lurked in the countryside, and the Lord of Misrule was tied into the medieval Christmas anarchy which had long since subsided. But Santa Claus was free to embody the Christmas principles of the modern era and become a gift-bringer for the nineteenth century. If the Christmas that the English and American urban middle classes aspired to was a time of merriment, sentimentality, the family and gift-giving, Santa Claus was perfectly placed to embody those ideals. And the mythology was magical and exciting enough to have appeal far beyond that core demographic.

Santa Claus's legend spread over the next seventy years and by the late 1800s he was a common figure in children's songs and stories, featured on Christmas cards and in children's toys and games. In 1890 a man named James Edgar, who owned a department store in Massachusetts, decided to wear a Santa Claus outfit in the late afternoons near Christmas and thus created America's first department store Santa. In 1897 an eight-year-old girl's letter to the *New York Sun* questioning Santa's existence resulted in the article 'Yes, Virginia, There Is a Santa Claus', in which the newspaper, and its journalist Francis Church, assured Virginia that Santa Claus was a real figure and that all children should believe in him.

The Americans had succeeded in moving Christmas traditions away from the rowdy, drunken rioting and mumming of the beginning of the century, and had created a festive figure for all the family. For better or worse, Christmas had been reinvented and Santa Claus had arrived.

10

The Coca-Cola Santa?

Santa Claus (America and the World)

Two hundred years on from Diedrich Knickerbocker, Santa Claus has become one of the most recognisable characters in the world. His popularity and the impact of his constant media appearances is such that many of the European Christmas figures I have discussed in the book have found themselves becoming more Santa-like. Some, like Sinterklaas and the Three Kings, have held on to their identity but become gentler and more child-friendly. Others have effectively turned into Santa. This has been an easier process for some than others. Father Christmas, Père Noël and the Weinnachtsmann were already so Santa-like for the transition to be scarcely noticeable. But the Yule Lads, the tomte and Joulupukki have undergone complete transformations in behaviour and appearance to be more like the man in red. To many people, St Nicholas and Santa Claus are now synonymous. Even in countries like Japan and Thailand, where Christians make up less than 1 per cent of the population, Santa Claus has become a hugely popular figure.

However, he is also divisive. Many people blame him for eradicating local customs and see him as a tool of US global capitalism. In *Rare Exports*, the 2010 Finnish film that connects the modern-day Santa Claus with the Sami mythology of the lethal child-murdering Staalo, a character dismissively refers to him as not the real Santa but 'the Coca-Cola Santa'.

This phrase refers to one of the most pervasive and frequent criticisms of Santa Claus – namely that he is such a shill of big business that even his red suit comes from Coca-Cola. The story goes that Santa Claus was originally green until the 1930s, when the Coca-Cola marketing board, anxious to promote their soft drink with the help of the jolliest Christmas figure of them all, changed the colour of his suit to red in order to match the colour of their cans.

This is a commonly repeated tale and anyone with the vaguest interest in the history of Santa Claus will have heard it. But is it true? The one-word answer is 'no'. Santa Claus has never been exclusively, or even predominantly, depicted in green, although many early images of Father Christmas in England did have him adorned with holly and shrubbery. Santa Claus frequently appeared in red long before Coca-Cola used him in their advertising. There is a 1911 postcard of Santa Claus leaving the 'St Nicholas Toy Emporium' which shows a very familiar image of Santa with red clothes and black boots, about to be tripped up by two naughty children. Even before that, an 1886 children's book called *Santa Claus' Visit to the Schoolroom* shows Santa in red. Even the 1821 *Children's Friend* book about St Nicholas shows the man in red in some of the pictures. By the 1930s, Santa was already a predominantly red character.

Thomas Nast

But where does the image of Santa Claus come from? And why do we think Coca-Cola invented it?

To take the first question first, Santa Claus had no set image until the nineteenth century. Sometimes he would be wearing rags, sometimes furs and sometimes tweed. Red, green and brown were the most common colours for his clothes but they really could be any colour you liked. In one nineteenth-century postcard he is clad all in white and entertaining a pretty young woman in stockings and a chemise. Like his appearance, Santa's behaviour was not yet set in stone.

The person usually credited with creating the image of Santa Claus we know today was Thomas Nast, the cartoonist at the influential *Harper's Weekly* magazine in New York. Nast's father was a Protestant from the traditionally Catholic German state of Bavaria who had fled to New York for political reasons when the boy was six years old. Nast's drawings embodied both the way that old Catholic traditions of St Nicholas were being rapidly reimagined through Protestant eyes and also the way that traditions stemming from fourteenth-century Europe were reborn in the world of nineteenth-century America.

Nast's first image of the character that came to be embraced as Santa Claus appeared on the front cover of *Harper's Weekly* in December 1862. It was the height of the Civil War and a low point for the North, who had suffered heavy losses at the Battle of Fredericksburg only a few weeks before Christmas. Nast was a fervent supporter of the war and the battle against slavery, but drew an image to reflect his sadness at the separation and loss that the war caused in ordinary families. Nast, who had spent time in England, may have been influenced by the way that Father Christmas had developed as an expression of sadness for lost Christmas traditions and of hope for a better future. He drew a powerful, striking image of despair as a wife sits praying at her window whilst her children lie in bed. Many miles away sits a weary, ageing solider. He has the beard and rotund figure that was already familiar in the pictures of the Christmas Men and would soon be known around the world as Santa Claus. But, far from being the joyful personification of Christmas, he slumps sadly with a letter in his hand. Even 150 years later, it is a heartbreaking image of longing, hope and loss. A year later, Nast drew the same figure again, this time clearly identifying him as Santa Claus. He is dressed in a Union flag and hands out presents to soldiers who are separated from their families.

After that, Nast continued to draw Santa for the next thirty years. Once the war was won he seemed to cheer up considerably and he gradually became the man we know and love today. Nast's German roots meant that he was aware of European folk mythology, and his residence in New York meant that he was also aware of the Clement Clarke Moore poem. Nast's drawings were the point where European traditions and Irving's and Moore's writings came together to create something new.

St Nicholas was no longer an austere saint but a jolly toymaker. His assistants were no longer angry, fearsome devils but friendly elves. He did not judge children but simply recorded their hopes and wishes in a giant ledger. He liked food being left out for him but he was not going to punish anyone who failed to leave him an offering. Nast was also the first person to encourage children to write to Santa and to locate Santa Claus's workshop at the North Pole. Nast's grandson Thomas Nast St Hill speculates that the reason for this was the combination of a neutral location, so that Santa could not be appropriated as a political figure by any particular country, and the fact that the North Pole made it easy for Santa Claus to access both the United States and Europe – even at this time Santa's status as a global gift-bringer was beginning to develop.[34]

Nast helped put European folklore back into the heart of Santa Claus, albeit in a much nicer and more child-friendly form than it had ever appeared before. In doing so, he helped ease the way for Santa to supersede the same myths he had been inspired by. It was through his drawings that Santa Claus became generally accepted as wearing red.

Nonetheless, there were still lots of people drawing Santa Claus in different colours and there was still freedom to interpret Santa as you saw fit. Towards the end of the nineteenth century, Santa Claus spread into Europe. England, where Father Christmas had never been influenced by St Nicholas at all, proved the most susceptible. In fact the first Christmas grotto in the UK opened in Lewis's store in Liverpool as early as 1879, a full eleven years before James Edgar's department store Santa in Massachusetts. Nast's decision to place Santa at the North Pole allowed him to gain popularity in Scandinavia and especially Finland. Children located near the Arctic and surrounded by snow and reindeer could easily believe the character was local to them.

By the 1920s the Finnish Broadcasting Company was broadcasting *Children's Hour with Uncle Markus* on the radio, a show that invented much of the Santa Claus mythology in Finland. Suddenly, Joulupukki was no longer a sinister goat but simply Santa Claus. If the mythology was easy to adopt, however, Santa Claus's image was confused – especially in countries where he had never been a man at all. The 1940s Swedish children's book *Peter and Lotta's Christmas* perhaps best sums up the confusion as the children are visited by a being that acts like Santa, but is half-man and half-goat. American influence might have been growing across Europe but Santa's image was still up for grabs.

You Can't Beat the Real Thing

This is where Coca-Cola came in. They were not the first company to use Santa to advertise products. Santa Claus was already a popular commercial figure. His image was used in children's books, toys and games, and he was already being used to advertise soap, cigarettes and a range of other products. However, nineteenth-century businesses advertised to their local areas only. Chain stores and national advertising were rare. An advert placed in New York would have no influence in Chicago and certainly would not reach to the wider world.

Over the twentieth century, big businesses became – for want of a better phrase – big business. Corporations now had a reach that extended far beyond their local communities. Advertising became coordinated nationally, or even internationally, and brands began to be famous. The development of the automobile saw a huge increase in the road network, whilst the development of major highways led to the invention of billboards visible to passing motorists. Before, adverts were small-scale posters or inserts in the local newspaper. Now advertising was literally huge.

Contrary to popular mythology, it is likely that Coca-Cola chose Santa Claus because he was normally depicted in red, rather than the other way round. Certainly the artist Haddon Sundblom was heavily influenced by the illustrations of Thomas Nast. Sundblom made Santa a little rounder, perhaps a little more cheerful and a little friendlier. He also made him a full-size figure, not the elfin creature of Clement Clarke Moore's imagination. But the main power of the image Sundblom created was that the Coca-Cola adverts featured heavily on billboards every year from 1931 onwards for the next thirty years. The cumulative effect of this advertising meant that – not only in America but in Europe too – the image of Santa Claus finally became defined and inescapable. To children everywhere, Sundblom's picture *was* Santa Claus.

Despite Coca-Cola not quite having invented Santa Claus, there is one famous aspect of Santa's mythology that does have its roots in purely commercial decision-making. In the 1930s an

213

American chain of department stores called Montgomery Ward were buying and giving away free colouring books to children each year. This was an expensive business and in 1939, to save money, they hired one of their advertising copywriters, a man called Robert L. May, to design a storybook of their own. May wrote a story about Santa's much-mocked ninth reindeer. The book was popular and ten years later May's brother-in-law turned the story into a song. Half a century later, 'Rudolph the Red-Nosed Reindeer' remains a popular part of Christmas mythology.

Santa Claus and the Movies

Coca-Cola proudly boast of their part in the history of Santa Claus on their website but they cannot take all the credit for the popularity of the character. Another force, more powerful even than Coca-Cola, has been instrumental in first creating and then disseminating the homogenised image of the modern Santa Claus around the world. If the nineteenth century saw the first mass-produced pictures and postcards being shared around the world, the twentieth century saw the spread of the moving image. As Hollywood dominated global cinema, and US television networks exported their shows all over the world, children everywhere became acquainted with the image of Santa Claus.

Santa was a popular subject from the very first days of cinema. Three very early short films showed him in action. *Santa Claus Filling Stockings* (1897) was literally exactly what you would assume from the title, and *Santa Claus and the Children* (1898) was equally descriptive. In 1899 *The Visit from Santa Claus* showed our hero filling stockings and disappearing up the chimney. Even before the nineteenth century had ended, film was implanting Santa mythology firmly in children's imaginations.

214

By 1910 the story of Santa Claus was so well known that film-makers were starting to subvert it. D.W. Griffiths made a film about children hoping to trap Santa Claus, who inadvertently foiled their evil estranged father's attempts at burglary, and a 1914 film called *The Wrong Santa Claus* shows another wicked burglar pretending to be Santa to steal all the toys.

By the middle of the twentieth century Santa Claus was a regular fixture in films – *Babes in Toyland* (1934), *Miracle on 34th Street* (1947), *Santa Claus* (1960) – and regularly appeared as a guest character on TV shows. L. Frank Baum, J.R.R. Tolkien and C.S. Lewis had all featured Father Christmas in stories, and he was used in television adverts and posters to sell everything from shredded wheat and soap to fountain pens.

What's more, songs were being written about the jolly man in red. 'Here Comes Santa Claus' (1947) merely spread the prevailing image about Santa, whilst 'Santa Claus Is Coming to Town' (1934) linked the character back to St Nicholas's threats about punishing naughty children. Chuck Berry and the Beach Boys released songs that gave Santa a sheen of rock'n'roll cool credibility and in 1953 Eartha Kitt even turned the roly-poly septuagenarian into a sex symbol.

Santa entered other areas of popular culture too. In 1937 Charles Howard opened the first Santa Claus school in New York, where students could get a Bachelor of Santa Claus, thus professionally qualifying them as department store Santas. Santa costumes were also popular with charity fundraisers. However, in 1937 the Salvation Army banned its volunteers from dressing as Santa Claus as they feared that children seeing lots of Santas together would make them suspect that the 'real' Santa Claus was just a man dressed up too. Santa was everywhere.

Santa Claus takes over the World

Over the twentieth century a pattern was repeated from country to country as existing Christmas myths were gradually superseded by a red-cloaked, white-bearded man. Often this new Santa Claus kept some of the traditions of his predecessor – the Weinnachtsmann and Père Noël, for example, were close enough to the figure that emerged in the USA that they only really needed a change of outfit and a home at the North Pole to merge seamlessly into the American character. In other countries the leap was far more substantial. Joulupukki in Finland and the tomte in Sweden went from goat and elf to man respectively, and only their names remain from their previous incarnations. In other countries Santa Claus's mythology merged with the previous folk mythologies. For example, the Yule Lads remained mischievous trolls who visited houses to play tricks before Christmas, but now they dressed in Santa suits, gave up frightening children and started handing out gifts instead.

Not all European myths were susceptible. St Nicholas and the Three Kings retained their individuality – even if they have acquired the gentleness and compassion associated with the 'real' Santa Claus. Sinterklaas is still extremely popular in the Netherlands, whilst Germany, Belgium, the Czech Republic and many other European countries celebrate St Nicholas's Day with a visit from the saint. However, they still face a problem – with children so acquainted with Santa from American culture, it leads to difficult questions as to why he does not visit their house. The result of this in recent years has been an increase in households where children receive two Christmas visitors, each of whom brings presents separately.

Other European mythologies have been untouched by the

invention of Santa Claus. Both the festive, drunken rampaging of the Krampus and the child-munching menace of the Christmas Cat are sufficiently separate from Santa to be untroubled by the man in red. Both continue to rampage regardless.

Nonetheless, Santa Claus is now popular all over the world. Part of this is because of the influence of colonialists and missionaries who brought Christianity and its traditions to the people of Africa and South America, but Santa Claus has even managed to become popular in countries that have no real relationship with Christianity at all.

Thailand is a Buddhist country where Christians are few and far between. Completely stripped from their religious context, Christmas decorations adorn department stores and hotels, with depictions of Santa Claus the most popular image of all. Thailand even prints scores of Christmas cards, humorously juxtaposing his fur-lined clothes and sleigh with the warm Thai climate. Santa appears as a hapless tourist, struggling to mount elephants or buffalos instead of his sleigh, frantically searching for directions and struggling to keep up with traditional Thai dancers.

Japan is another country that has passionately adopted Santa Claus, despite Christianity having no real foothold. As in Thailand, less than 1 per cent of Japanese are Christians, but the gift-giving side of Christmas is widely celebrated and they even have a Buddhist monk called Hotei-Osho, who is said to have eyes in the back of his head to witness children's behaviour, and who acts as a Santa figure. Nonetheless, Santa suits are extremely popular (for some reason especially so when they are worn by female anime characters) and he is a popular figure in cartoons, films and television. Mostly weirdly, KFC have managed to equate Colonel Sanders with Santa Claus and, in doing so, made fried chicken the traditional Japanese Christmas meal!

Believing in Santa Claus is now big business and Finland in particular has made the most of its proximity to the Arctic, its possession of parts of Lapland and an abundance of reindeer to brand itself as the home of Santa Claus. Korvatunturi, where Finnish people believe Santa Claus lives, is on the border of Finland and Russia and cannot be visited without permission from the Finnish border guards, so the Finnish have constructed the Santa Claus Village and Santa Park theme parks in Rovaniemi, around 500 kilometres to the south of Korvatunturi. These attractions boast around half a million visitors a year.

In recent years the town of North Pole, Alaska, has attempted to challenge Lapland's claim to be the 'official' home of St Nicholas. North Pole is actually about 1,700 miles south of the geographical North Pole but is nonetheless one of the most northern outposts in America. It has Christmas decorations up all year round. The journalist Jon Ronson says that the post office in North Pole receives letters each year that have been addressed to Santa Claus at the North Pole.[35] Replies are written by staff with help from the local middle school's eleven- or twelve-year-olds who take on elf names and write back on Santa's behalf. This can be traumatic for some children when they turn up in school and have a bundle of letters to answer which seem to conclusively prove that Santa Claus does not exist.

The only letters that reach Alaska, however, are the ones with a complete North Pole address and postcode – otherwise they are dealt with by local post offices. A 2006 survey found that six million letters are sent to Santa Claus each year, and five million volunteers across the world help sort through them. Santa Claus is a global celebrity.

The Anti-Santa Backlash

Santa's popularity comes at a price and he has attracted a backlash amongst those that feel he demeans the 'true meaning' of Christmas. In 2010 a group called Repent Amarillo made a video of themselves trying Santa Claus for 'false idolatry', 'polluting truth of Jesus Christ in the hearts of children' and 'turning Christmas into a festival of gluttony and greed with rampant commercialism', before literally subjecting an effigy of Santa Claus to death by firing squad. It's frightening stuff and they really do not seem to be joking.

Surprisingly, it is not the first time Santa Claus has been executed. In Dijon in 1951 Catholic clergymen at the city's cathedral, increasingly unhappy with Santa's influence, burned an effigy of him in front of their Sunday-school children. But why would anybody want Santa Claus dead?

The complaint of the bishops, one that Repent Amarillo seem to share, is that Santa Claus is responsible for taking Christianity out of Christmas. Japan and Thailand represent a version of Christmas that's entirely devoid of its religious aspects. This has caused some concern that Santa Claus distracts from the celebration of Christ's birth and instead promotes a Christmas that focuses purely on materialism and commercial greed.

On top of religious concerns, there has been a backlash from traditionalists trying to preserve their own festive rituals from the cultural domination of Santa Claus. In 1999 the National Museum of Iceland commissioned new outfits for the Yule Lads to distinguish them from Santa Claus. In the Czech Republic the Creative Copywriters Club have protested that the ubiquitous presence of Santa Claus compromises traditional Czech celebrations of St Nicholas and the Christ Child. And a Catholic group in Germany called for a Santa-Free Zone and produced badges and posters decrying Santa and demanding a return to the 'real' St Nicholas.

Their spokesman, German TV presenter Peter Hahne, said:

> St Nicholas is not Father Christmas. The values associated with the former are selflessness, charity, solidarity, giving and sharing. He is perfect for getting across the Christmas message.
>
> Santa Claus on the other hand is a product of a consumer society. He is a symbol of shopping and has got nothing to do with St Nicholas, who still teaches us today that giving does not make you poorer, but richer.[36]

Perhaps the accusation of promoting consumerism is the one that is levelled at Santa Claus the most. He has been accused of being used by toy companies to help increase demand for gifts for children, with many parents feeling a child's traditional letter to Santa is basically a shopping list for which the parent either must foot the bill or explain to their child why – perhaps even in spite of their good behaviour – Santa hasn't brought them what they wanted.

Save Our Santa

But for all the people who criticise Santa, there are far more that see him as an integral part of Christmas. In April 2005 Darren Cullen, a student at the Glasgow School of Art, decided to erect a billboard for an art project. The billboard was to read: 'Santa gives more to rich kids than poor kids. Stop lying to your children about Santa Claus.'

Cullen is not a fan of Santa and claims he teaches children to equate material possessions with happiness.

> Santa gets consumers when they're young, and gives them their first taste of what capitalism has to offer *them*. In later years they might discover brutal truths about the nature of the system, but they'll always have those childhood memories, the golden Xmas of years past, the smell of toys fresh out of the box . . .'[37]

Cullen is not alone in his feelings. What is surprising is that his art project made headlines all around the world. The *Sun* newspaper managed to get the original billboard company to refuse to put up the poster due to fear of adverse publicity and boldly proclaimed that 'The *Sun* Saves Santa'.[38] In actual fact, the poster eventually went up and ultimately it made headlines as far afield as the USA, South Africa, Pakistan and Bahrain. The fact that one poster by one student received so much attention shows how deeply ingrained Santa Claus is within our culture and how his identity is inextricably bound up with the idea of 'the magic of Christmas'.

In fact, attempts to present Santa as anything other than an innocent, pure children's hero can attract bad publicity. In recent years, Santa has been used for awareness campaigns that are definitely not aimed at children. In 2009 a charity in Bangkok constructed a model Santa Claus out of condoms to promote safe sex. In 2012 Citiwide, a New York organisation dedicated to reducing harm from drug use, released a video of Santa handing out gifts of free condoms and clean needles to combat HIV. In Britain in 2008 the British Pregnancy Advisory Service advised women to stock morning-after pills using a poster that showed a woman being seduced by the red-suited man who had just come down her chimney and which featured the slogan 'Santa comes but once a year ... but that's all it takes'.

These adverts have attracted criticism from those keen to protect the sanctity of Christmas. Mike Judge from the Christian Institute said that the morning-after pill campaign 'says Christmas is all about booze and sex'[39] (it's probably a good job he wasn't around in medieval times). Conservative bloggers described the Citiwide advert of Santa handing out needles and syringes as 'morally disturbing'[40] and a 'new low for New York'.[41]

Commercial advertisers have also received criticism for their depictions of Santa. A 2012 Samsung advert in America showed Mrs Claus placing a home-made video on Santa's phone and hinting it might distract him if he watched it on the sleigh. Bloggers and newspaper seemed uncomfortable with this linking of sex and Santa. The Media Research Center called it 'one Christmas image viewers could do without',[42] an online blogger claimed the advert would 'ruin your childhood',[43] whilst Adam Graham in the *Detroit News* called it the 'worst commercial of 2012' and complained that the advert 'forces us to confront the idea of Mrs Claus, as pure and wholesome a symbol of childhood innocence as there is, making a sex tape for Santa. Look, I'm not trying to deny Mr and Mrs Claus a healthy sex life. But they're *not real*, they're characters. And there's no reason to sexualise them.'[44]

Bad Santa

It seems many people believe that showing Santa Claus as anything other than a benign, jolly children's character shatters innocent dreams and shows a disrespect for tradition by sullying the image of a popular character. However, sullying Santa's image is almost as old as Santa Claus himself.

For a start, Santa has been depicted in countless cigarette advertisements: 'Christmas isn't Christmas without Murad cigarettes'; 'Pall Mall cigarettes guard against throat-scratch'; 'Everybody loves a good smoke at Christmas'. Whatever the message cigarette companies want to convey, Santa has been the messenger of choice. Alcohol too is one of Santa's advertising pleasures. Obviously everyone knows that Santa enjoys a sly tot of whisky when he drops by with the presents, but children would doubtless be shocked by the 1934 advert for Byrrh wine where Santa sits on a rooftop, swigging from a bottle and looking half-dead from intoxication. A beautiful angel kneels beside him and it is unclear whether she is joining in the fun or reading him the last rites. The image is supposed to suggest merry seasonal drinking, but looks more like an alcoholic at his lowest ebb. And what of the recent trend for Santa being used to sell sex? This too is old hat. A 1947 lingerie advert shows Santa cuddling up to a leggy blonde who is extremely keen to show off her purchases.

Sex, cigarettes and booze may paint Santa as a bit of a rogue but it is the gun adverts where it really gets disturbing. A 1950 advert shows Santa assuring parents the Winchester rifle is the best and safest choice to buy their son. A 1966 advert goes one stage further and sees Santa advising a boy to leave pictures of Remington guns on 'Dad's desk or Mom's vanity table' as a subtle Christmas hint. It handily adds, 'Remington ammunition makes a dandy Christmas present, too.' Of course, it is unwise to jump to conclusions. Just because Santa is advocating the purchase of guns doesn't mean anyone is going to get hurt – except in the 1947 advert for Arrow shirts, which shows Santa aiming a gun into his own mouth ready to end it all in despair at the number of shirts he has to deliver due to the anticipated surge in Arrow's sales. Merry Christmas, folks!

The Patron Saint of Christmas

These strange and inappropriate takes on Santa Claus might seem as though whoever designed them has completely missed the point of Santa. Indeed, Santa Claus is almost unique in terms of the number of ways he has been re-imagined and reinvented over the years. In fact, despite his perceived homogeneity, Santa has succeeded by being an extremely adaptable figure. Every country might agree he lives near the North Pole and flies on a sleigh pulled by reindeer giving presents to children, but his personality and lifestyle are vague and malleable. The Thai, the Japanese, the Finnish or the English can all flavour him with their own customs and put their own spin on the character without losing the essence of Santa.

With similar ease, corporations and advertisers can adapt him to be what they want him to be in the knowledge that customers will think positively of Santa and, by extension, their product too. Santa Claus can simultaneously be a poster boy for capitalism, a Christian figure, a crusader for social justice and a symbol of Christmas tradition with very little contradiction.

How can one character be represented in so many ways?

The spread of Santa across America and Europe is not dissimilar from the way missionaries originally spread Christianity by assimilating and integrating Christian beliefs into existing myths. There were so few concrete facts about Santa that people were able to shape the character to be whatever they liked.

Just as St Nicholas could be adopted as the patron saint of

both judges and murderers, both the married and the unmarried, both businessmen and the destitute, and both the clergy and prostitutes, so Santa Claus's history is rich in ideas but sparse on detail, so anyone who wants him can use him to represent what they want. With the slightest of tweaks, Santa can be a modern take on St Nicholas, the contemporary equivalent of Odin's Wild Hunt, the symbol of Father Christmas's struggle against the Puritans, a Protestant Christmas Man or a new slant on the mystical elves and demons that haunted the European midwinter. Perhaps this flexibility, rather than gift-giving itself, is St Nicholas's greatest gift to his modern-day descendant.

Santa Claus, especially now he has been stripped of his bishop's robes and medieval mythology, is so flexible he can be whatever people choose to make him. The 'facts' we know about him are few and the myths and legends are numerous, so we shape him as we want. Santa is a blank canvas on which each society paints their values. Advertisers use him so frequently because we associate him with positive qualities, but people do not necessarily agree on what those qualities are.

He is a man who can be a protector of children, punisher of those who misbehave, a defender of Christmas traditions, a patron saint of religion, a wild man of paganism, a proponent of capitalism and a figure of charity and kindness.

Santa Claus has survived and thrived by being all things to all people.

Conclusion

The Patron Saint of Christmas

Over the last century, Santa Claus has become an all-conquering image of Christmas, incorporating and superseding myths from Europe to become popular with the religious and irreligious alike.

Who Is Santa Claus?

But what makes him different from the European Christmas characters of the past? Russell Belk, a professor at the University of Utah, points out five things that make Santa distinct from his predecessors.[45] I've summarised his points and added my own thoughts below each one.

1. Unlike St Nicholas, the Christkind or the Three Kings, Santa Claus is not a religious figure.

Figures like Odin or Saturn were popular amongst pagans but rejected by Christians due to their association with pre-Christian rituals. Creatures like the Krampus, Zwarte Piet, Schmutzli and

Joulupukki were also believed to have roots in pagan rituals and, at the height of the witch trials, to be symbols of the Devil.

St Nicholas has always been popular amongst Catholics and many Orthodox Christians but was rejected by Protestants after the Reformation due to their lack of belief in the veneration of saints and eschewed by non-Christians on account of his religious associations.

A figure like the Christkind could have been accepted by all Christians at least, but failed to win over those who did not believe in Christianity. What's more, many Catholics would have objected to the figure because of its Protestant connotations.

Santa Claus is a Protestant update of a Catholic tradition. Protestants could accept him because he was not depicted as a saint. Catholics could accept him because he was – in name and action – an update of St Nicholas. What's more, he has parallels with Odin and pagan rituals but, as he is not an overtly religious character, he can also appeal to non-believers and even to people in countries with no history of Christianity.

In short, he is an entirely flexible figure who can be as religious or irreligious as you want him to be.

His ease of adoption in Europe was also helped by the fact that a number of other Protestant 'Christmas Men' rose up in England, France and Germany at a similar time to Santa Claus. However, whilst the possibility of creating new myths around them was hampered by the weight of existing traditions around St Nicholas, America was far enough removed from European folklore to take inspiration from it without being wedded to it. Without the history of the early figures, it was easy for Irving to add the touch of climbing down a chimney, Clement Clarke Moore to assign reindeer and Nast to give him a workshop at the North Pole. Thus a new mythology was born.

2. Unlike the Lord of Misrule or the Krampus, Santa Claus is not a figure of chaos or anarchy.

From the time of Yule, January Kalends and Saturnalia through to the Middle Ages, midwinter celebrations were focused around drinking and partying to celebrate the end of harvest and to relieve the boredom of winter, mixed in with rituals of social equality and role-reversal to act as a respite for the poor from their suffering and for the rich from their need to maintain social appearances.

Nonetheless, the close association with the harvest and the agricultural calendar made it an essentially rural festival. As people moved to cities and winter working hours increased due to the Industrial Revolution, this aspect of the festival lost its relevance, especially as a middle class rose up that wanted to appear respectable and, as such, wanted Christmas celebrations that were removed from the drunken debauchery of the past.

In the nineteenth century Christmas became an urban middle-class festival. Santa Claus was created as a fun but civilised figure to embody the way to enjoy a jolly Christmas season without losing social respectability.

3. Unlike Sinterklaas, Zwarte Piet, Perchta, the Krampus or Staalo, Santa Claus does not punish people.

Historically winter has been a dangerous time where failure to obey rules and instructions could lead to death. Parents needed to ensure children stayed in at night and did not wander off alone, whilst societies needed to ensure parents provided their children with clothes and took steps to feed them and keep them warm. As a result, Christmas monsters were created that ate children or travellers alone at night, Christmas visitors were created that punished people who did not eat certain meals and the Christmas Cat was created that took away the children of neglectful parents who failed to clothe their offspring.

Furthermore, religious beliefs and superstitions were stronger and parents believed there was a real possibility of their children – especially in a time of high infant mortality – suffering eternal damnation. St Nicholas and his sinister assistants existed to make sure that children learned the Bible from an early age, as well as ensuring they were 'good' and followed their parents' instructions, which could save their lives. The cruelty of the Christmas visitors of the Middle Ages was a measure to save souls and lives.

As the literal belief in Hell subsided, and as winters became a little safer, this focus on obedience and punishment ceased to be necessary. What's more, in moving away from the anarchic drunken Christmases, the English and Americans of the nineteenth century invented a Christmas that was family-centred, with a focus on using the new-found wealth of the middle-classes to treat and spoil children. Santa Claus emphasises this desire to treat children and fulfil their wishes.

4. Santa Claus is a more visible figure, appearing on street corners, in department stores and at shopping malls. Despite having his home at the North Pole, his physical presence makes it far easier for him to capture children's imaginations than for the European Christmas characters.

I do not wholly agree with Belk on this point. Whilst it is true that Santa Claus is a very visible figure (and the fact he is depicted as a man rather than a monster makes him far easier to play convincingly), Sinterklaas and his assistants were visible too. The Krampusse too can still be seen charging through the streets of Austria each Christmas. In the Netherlands it is now as easy to visit Sinterklaas as it is to visit Santa Claus in England or America, although of course this is because of the influence of Santa Claus.

The real difference between Santa Claus and the European characters is that children would wait for Sinterklaas and his assistants to visit them, whereas they can physically choose to go and visit Santa Claus at his grotto. The fact that a visit to Santa involves a physical trip (and often a queue) adds to the sense of excitement and anticipation and turns it into an adventure.

5. Santa Claus brings substantial toys and gifts, unlike Sinterklaas and his compatriots who tended to bring fruit, nuts and small home-made items.

Again, this is a result of the nineteenth-century reinvention of Christmas and of an affluent middle class looking to spoil their children. The fact that Santa Claus brings children generous gifts – and indeed that, thanks to Thomas Nast, children can write letters to him and tell him what they want – increases the significance of Santa Claus in children's lives. After all, it is hard not to feel affection for someone who showers you with generous gifts and expects nothing in return!

The True Meaning of Christmas

The focus on Santa Claus as a figure of Christmas has attracted criticism both from people who feel his presence detracts from a festival that's about the birth of Christ and people who feel Christmas has become all about commercialism. You will often hear people say that we have lost the 'true meaning of Christmas'.

It is important to bear in mind that the idea of Christmas being better in the past is not new, as Simon Carter noted in 'Christmas Past, Christmas Present':

'Christmas isn't what it used to be'. Charles Dickens, in the *Pickwick Papers*, told us so in 1837. Washington Irving told us so in 1820. In 1730 an anonymous author, in the persona of Old Father Christmas, reminded us of the fact in 'Christmas Entertainments' and way back in 1631 Thomas Taylor mourned the days when Christmas hospitality really was true hospitality. 'Ask your Grandmother – Christmas was always better in the past.'[46]

Moreover, the idealised Christmas of devoted spiritual worship with an absence of commercialism has never actually existed. Even in the fourth century, as Christmas was first taking over from January Kalends, bishops like Asterius were denouncing the festival for encouraging excess and materialism. As Catholicism established its foothold around Europe, celebrations were mixed in with leftover pagan and Roman rituals involving masks, strange monsters and rituals to give thanks for the harvest and ensure a good crop the following year. No sooner had the Church tried to stamp these out than the Reformation led to questions about how Christmas should be celebrated and whether it should even be celebrated at all. Christmas became a muted celebration in Protestant Europe – and one that was not celebrated at all in much of America – until the nineteenth century. When it was revived, people were already yearning for a Christmas past that never actually existed. We certainly have not lost the 'true meaning of Christmas' because we never had it in the first place!

What's more, Christmas has never been just about Christianity. As the attempts to abolish it in England, Scotland and Russia have shown, it is also about the need for a midwinter celebration to banish the misery of the 'dreadful cold' and to celebrate the passing of the worst part of the year and the journey towards the return of spring. That is not to dismiss the Christian claim on Christmas – over 1,600 years it has grown to be a key part of the Christian calendar and Christians have as valid a claim on the season as anyone else. But the idea that Christmas should *only* be for religion and the memory of Christ ignores the fact that people have a historical claim on it for a host of other reasons too.

Ultimately, Christmas is a flexible festival that has come to mean whatever any society wishes it to mean and the people celebrating it choose it to mean. This flexibility has been reflected in the Christmas figures that people create too. Societies focused around agriculture and the end of the harvest created pagan goats and monsters like the Joulupukki. Societies that focused on the need to obey rules to keep safe invented the Staalo and the Christmas Cat. Societies that focused on religious obedience and avoiding Hell created the Sinterklass of medieval times, and societies that were based on a strict hierarchy created the Feast of Fools and the Lord of Misrule.

So what of Santa Claus? What does he represent?

To some, Santa Claus is the personification of joy and innocence at Christmas time; to others he represents the worst excesses of American hegemony and unfettered capitalism. He can be a symbol of charity or a symbol of greed, a symbol of Christianity or a symbol of pagan customs remaining in Christmas. Despite being designed as a respectable figure for middle-class audiences in America, he has spread all around the world and become everything from a bemused Western tourist in Thailand to an anime superhero in Japan, to the personification of the UK's traditional Christmas, to a thirteen-strong band of mischievous Yule Elves. He has advertised everything from toys and games to condoms and guns, and has been portrayed as a jolly figure of fun, a lovable old grouch or the thief who stole Christmas from Christianity.

Much like Christmas, he represents whatever you want him to.

This sounds facile but it is absolutely essential for Santa Claus's survival and popularity. In an increasingly globalised world, where Christmas celebrations differ from country to country and – even within each country – beliefs and traditions wildly differ, Santa Claus has retained a flexible enough mythology to change with the times and adapt to individual beliefs by embodying whatever we choose Christmas to mean.

People who love Christmas tend to love him, people who hate Christmas tend to dislike him; and he simultaneously embodies all that is good and all that is bad about the festive season. Indeed, he has become the embodiment of Christmas itself.

Christmas Future

At the same time I think it would be a mistake to assume that Santa Claus's domination of Christmas is fixed and will last forever. Every child grows up thinking the way they have celebrated Christmas is the way it *should* be celebrated and every generation believes that their tradition, their attitudes and their society will last forever. Every generation is subsequently proved wrong.

But Christmas's flexibility has allowed it to change and adapt to society for 1,600 years and there is no sign of it dying out in the foreseeable future. And what of Santa? The ubiquity of the character suggests he too will be around for a while yet but it seems likely that, over time, the number of countries that have adopted Santa will also find ways to change him to fit in with their own culture. But, as frustration grows with the omnipresence of American culture – and especially if a true backlash against global capitalism occurs or the US loses power and influence over the twenty-first century as the UK did across the twentieth, both of which seem to be real possibilities – it is easy to picture a resurgence of local Christmas characters.

Indeed, the Yule Lads have struck out for individualism in recent years and the popularity of the Krampus seems to be greater than ever. The days of the creepy Christmas characters may not yet have passed and the dark wintry figures that once stalked European forests at Christmas time may once again return to displace Santa.

Or who knows what weird and wonderful creatures might rise up instead?

Happy Christmas to all, and to all a Good Night.

Acknowledgements

Thanks to:

My parents – Colin and Janet Hawkins – for proofreading, advice (sometimes advice related to the book!) and general support.

Paul Finlay for giving me the advice and contacts that ultimately led to this book happening.

My agent Matthew Hamilton and my commissioning editor Kerri Sharp.

The following people for sharing their advice and experiences around Christmas traditions in specific countries: Kevin Hawkins, Kate Langley, Juha Niesniemi, William Vaughan, Gudjon Olaffson, Mary Boeker, Misha Chylkova.

Chris Potter, Jeremy Walton and Felix Hunt (as well as Juha and Mary) for letting me enthusiastically rant and rave at them whenever I found something new and exciting!

Jamie Beckwith Wilches for an array of history books on weird and wonderful subjects that convinced me a book like this might be possible.

ACKNOWLEDGEMENTS

And, finally, the numerous hobbyists and enthusiasts around the Internet who keep blogs and websites about Christmas traditions in their own countries. Their work is essential in preserving these stories, sharing them and keeping them alive.

Selected Bibliography

Aikio, Annukka and Samuli Aikio, *Lentonoidan poika. Saamelaisia satuja*, W. Soderstrom, 1978

Andersen, A., 'Icelandic Christmas through the ages', Reykjavic Grapevine, 03/01/11, http://www.grapevine.is/Features/Read Article/Slice-of-Icelandic-Christmas-Through-the-Ages

Asian Tribune, 'Santa Claus receives more than 6 million letters annually – and growing', http://www.asiantribune.com/node/8798, 20/12/07

Asterius of Amasea, *Sermons (1904)*. *Preface to the online edition*, Roger Pearse (translator), 2003

Baker, M., *Discovering Christmas Customs and Folklore*, Shire Publications, 1992

Beattie, A., *The Alps: A Cultural History (Landscapes of the Imagination)*, Signal Books, 2006

Beskow, E., *Peter and Lotta's Christmas*, Floris Books, 1947

Bowles, G., *The World Encyclopaedia of Christmas*, McClelland and Stewart, 2000

Brand, J. and Ellis, H., *The Popular Antiquities of Great Britain Largely Extended, Corrected, Brought Down To The Present Time, and Now First Alphabetically Arranged*, Reeves and Turner, 1905

Brendemoen, B., *The Turkish Dialects of Trabozon: An Analysis, Volumes 1–2*, Harrassowitz, 2002

Carter, S., *Christmas Past, Christmas Present: Four Hundred Years of English Seasonal Customs 1600–2000*, Geffrye Museum, 1997

Chambers, E.K., *The Medieval Stage*, Oxford University Press, 1903

The Children's Society website, http://www.childrenssociety.org.uk/what-you-can-do/fundraising-and-appeals/christingle/what-christingle

Christos, 'Kallikantzoros' Shadowness.com, http://shadowness.com/Christos/kallikantzaros-2

Cohen, E., *Explorations in Thai Tourism*, Emerald Publishing, 2008

Connelly, M., *Christmas: A Social History*, I.B. Tauris, 1999

Connelly, M., *Christmas at the Movies: Images of Christmas in American, British and European Cinema*, I.B. Tauris, 2000

Count, E.W. & Count, A.L., *4000 Years of Christmas*, Ullyses, 1997

Crichton, R., *Who is Santa Claus? The true story behind a living legend*, Canongate, 1987

'Czech Folks' blog, http://czechfolks.com/2008/12/06/dec-6th---st-nicholas-day/

'Czech Mate' blog, http://czechmatediary.com/2012/12/11/st-nicholas-day-at-our-house-part-i/

Davidson, H.E., 'The Wild Hunt', in Davidson, H. and Chaudhri, A., *Supernatural Enemies*, Carolina Academic Press, 2001

DW.com, 'Santa Again in Sights of Anti-Commercialisation Group' 21/12/08 http://www.dw.de/santa-again-in-sights-of-anti-commercialism-group/a-3893481

Father Flog, Humoristic Publishing Co, Kansas City, c. 1860

Forbes, B.D., *Christmas: A Candid History*, University of California Press 2007

Frazer, J.G., *The Golden Bough, 3rd Edition Part VI: the Scapegoat*, Macmillian & Co, 1913

Friends of the Caganer website, http://www.amicsdelcaganer.cat/

Golby, J.M. and Purdue, A.W., *The Making of the Modern Christmas*, B.T. Batsford Ltd, 1986

Grossman, J., *Christmas Curiosities: Odd, Dark and Forgotten Christmas*, Stewart, Tabori and Chang, 2008

Guerber, H.A., *Myths of the Norsemen*, George C. Harrap 1998

Haid, O., 'Christmas Markets in the Tyrolean Alps: Representing

Regional Traditions in a Newly Created World of Christmas' in Picard, D. and Robinson, M., *Festivals, Tourism and Social Change Remaking Worlds*, 2006

Harding, P., *The Magic of Christmas*, Metro Publishing, 2004

Harris, M., *Sacred Folly: A New History of the Feast of Fools*, Cornell University Press 2011

Irvine, I., 'Btw', the *Independent,* 26/11/05, http://www.independent.co.uk/voices/commentators/ian-irvine-btw-516988.html

Jackson, S. *The Medieval Christmas*, Sutton Publishing, Stroud, 2005

Jones, Rev. C.W., *St Nicholas of Myra, Bari and Manhatten*, University of Chicago, 1978

Jones, Rev. D.K., *The Real Father Christmas: The Truth Behind the Legend*, Heart of Oak, 2005

Jonnson, Vignir, 'The Yule Cat', http://www.simnet.is/gardarj/yule 11.htm

Joynes, A., *Medieval Ghost Stories: An Anthology of Miracles, Marvels And Prodigies*, Boydell Press, 2001

Keller, M., *The Art and Politics of Thomas Nast*, Oxford University Press, 1968

www.krampus.com

Lamb, R., 'War on Christmas? What about the War on Krampus?' 21/12/12, http://www.stufftoblowyourmind.com/blog/war-on-krampus/

LeBouthillier, E., 'The Wild Hunt', Eurofolk Asatru Community Association website, 2008, http://www.socalasatru.org/Dec08_00.html

Lending, J., www.livius.org

Lévi-Strauss, C., 'Santa Claus Executed' (1952) in *Unwrapping Christmas*, pp. 38–51, edited by D. Miller, Clarendon Press, 1993

Lyon, K., 'Santa's Little Helper – Schmutzli', Two Fools Zurich, 2012, http://www.twofoolszuerich.com/2009/12/santas-little-helper-schmutzli.html

Lysaght, P., 'The Wild Hunt in the Sea: Stories from the South-West of Ireland' in Davidson, H. and Chaudhri, A., *Supernatural Enemies*, Carolina Academic Press, 2001

Macrae, F., 'Is this crude ad really the best way to tackle unwanted pregnancies?' the *Daily Mail*, 28/11/08, http://www.dailymail.co.uk/femail/article-1090080/Is-crude-ad-really-best-way-tackle-unwanted-pregnancies-Christmas.html#ixzz2TRGQZ85V

Marling, K.A., *Christmas: Celebrating America's Greatest Holiday*, Harvard University Press, 2000

Merck, R.M., *Deck the Halls*, Abeville Press Publishers, 1992

Miall, A. and P., *The Victorian Christmas Book*, Dent, 1978

Miles, C.A., *Christmas in Ritual and Tradition, Christian and Pagan*, Adelphi Terrace, 1913

McKnight, George H., *St Nicholas*, New York: Knickerbocker, 1917, quoted in Siefker, P., *Santa Claus, Last of the Wild Men: The Origins and Evolution of Saint Nicholas, Spanning 50,000 Years*, McFarland, 1997

McLean, M., 'Schmutzli: The Swiss Santa's Sinister Sidekick', The Swiss Broadcasting Corporation's International Service, 05/12/08, http://www.swissinfo.ch/eng/Schmutzli:_the_Swiss_Santas_sinister_sidekick.html?cid=7082046

Morottaja, M., 'The Storytelling Tradition', Sami Museum website, 2006, http://www.samimuseum.fi/anaras/english/kieli/kertoma perinne.html

Nast, T. and Nast St Hill, T., *Thomas Nast's Christmas Drawings*, Dover Publications, 1978

National Museum of Iceland, http://www.thjodminjasafn.is/english/for-visitors/christmas/the-yule-lads/ retrieved 24/01/12

Nissenaum, S., *The Battle for Christmas*, Alfred A. Knopf, 1966

Paxman, J., *Empire: What Ruling the World Did to the British*, Viking, 2012

Plutarch, *The Parallel Lives*, Loeb Classical Library Edition, Volume VII, 1919, reproduced at http://penelope.uchicago.edu/Thayer/E/Roman/Texts/Plutarch/Lives/Caesar*.html

Rainsford, S., 'A Traditional Nativity Scene, Catalan Style', BBC News, 23/12/10, http://www.bbc.co.uk/news/world-europe-12059969

Ronson, J., 'Santa's Little Conspirators' in *Lost At Sea: The Jon Ronson Mysteries*, Picador, 2012

St Nicholas Center website, www.stnicholascenter.com

'Serendipity by an Ethnologist' blog http://serendipitybyanethnologist-helena.blogspot.co.uk/2012/12/joulustaalo_17.html

Sevhla, G.J. and Sevhla, S., *It's Christmas Time at the Movies*, Midnight Marquee Press, 1998

Sexton, T., 'Kallikantzoros – True Story of the Legendary Mythical Christmas Goblin', Yahoo.com, 21/09/09, http://voices.yahoo.com/kallikantzaroi-true-story-legend-the-4278393.html,

Shetland.org, 'Shetland Christmas Past', http://move.shetland.org/shetland-christmas-past

Siefker, P., *Santa Claus, Last of the Wild Men: The Origins and Evolution of Saint Nicholas, Spanning 50,000 Years*, McFarland, 1997

Siida.Fi, 'Joulustallo', http://www.siida.fi/sisalto/lapsille-ja-opiskeli-joille/vuodenajan-teema/arkisto/joulustaalo

'Sinterklaas Canada', http://www.sinterklaas.ca/

Steves, R. and Griffiths, V., *Rick Steves' European Christmas*, Avalon Travel Publishing, 2005

Towrie, S., Orkneyjar.com, http://www.orkneyjar.com/tradition/hunt.htm

Tulloch, L., *The Foy and Other Folk Tales*, Shetland Books, 2007

Turi, J., *Turi's Book of Lapland*, translated into Danish by Emilie Demant Hatt and from Danish by E. Gee Hash, Jonathan Cape, 1931

Wagner, A., 'Perchtenläufe: Salzburg's Pagan Heritage', Visit Salzburg website, http://www.visit-salzburg.net/travel/perchten.htm

Ward. C., 'Ten Fun Facts about the Krampus, the Christmas Demon', Topless Robot, 23/12/10, http://www.toplessrobot.com/2010/12/10_fun_facts_about_krampus_the_christmas_demon.php

Warner, M., *Monsters of Our Own Making: The Peculiar Pleasures of Fear*, University Press of Kentucky, 1998

Wernecke, Herbert H., *Christmas Customs around the World*, Bailey Brothers and Swinfen Ltd, 1999

Woodhead, I., 'Babushka and the Three Kings: A Christmas Tale but not Russian', Suite 101, 25/03/13, http://suite101.com/article/babushka-and-the-three-kings—-a-christmas-tale-but-not-russian-a313464

Zawadil, A., 'Santa's evil sidekick gives jolly fright to kids', Reuters.com, 07/12/06, http://uk.reuters.com/article/2006/12/07/lifestyle-austria-christmas-devil-dc-idUKL0438534320061207

Zurich Expats, http://zurichexpats.com/schmutzli-bad-santa-switzerland/

Notes and References

CHAPTER ONE

1 Myra itself was abandoned at sometime around the eleventh century but the town of Demre now stands in its place.
2 For example, Charles W. Jones, *St Nicholas of Myra, Bari and Manhatten*, University of Chicago, 1978.
3 Jones, Rev. D.K., The Real Father Christmas: The Truth Behind the Legend, Jersey, 2005; p.6.
4 McKnight. George H., *St Nicholas*, Knickerbocker, 1917, quoted in Siefker, P. *The Origins and Evolution of Saint Nicholas, Spanning 50,000 Years*, McFarland, 1997.

CHAPTER THREE

5 The date of this is disputed. Marina Warner (in *Monsters of Our Own Making: The Peculiar Pleasures of Fear*, University Press of Kentucky, 1998) gives the date of the Humoristic Publishing Company cartoon as around 1930 but some online sources date it at around 1860. Warner is an award-winning historian and mythographer and so seems the most trustworthy source.
6 Siefker, P., The Origins and Evolution of Saint Nicholas, Spanning 50,000 Years, McFarland, 1997.

NOTES AND REFERENCES

7   McLean, M., 'Schmutzli: The Swiss Santa's Sinister Sidekick', The Swiss Broadcasting Corporation's International Service, 05/12/08, http://www.swissinfo.ch/eng/Schmutzli:_the_Swiss_Santas_sinister_sidekick.html?cid=7082046

8   Hugger, P., in McLean, M., ibid.

9   Zawadil, A., 'Santa's Evil Sidekick? Who Knew?' Reuters, 06/12/06, http://www.reuters.com/article/2006/12/06/us-austria-christmas-devil-idUSL0438534320061206

10 Haid, O., 'Christmas Markets in the Tyrolean Alps: Representing Regional Traditions in a Newly Created World of Christmas' in Picard, D. and Robinson, M., *Festivals, Tourism and Social Change Remaking Worlds*, 2006

CHAPTER FOUR

11 Miles, C.A., Christmas in Ritual and Tradition, Christian and Pagan, Adelphi Terrace, 1913.

12 Towrie, S., Orkneyjar.com, http://www.orkneyjar.com/tradition/hunt.htm

13 LeBouthillier, E., 'The Wild Hunt', Eurofolk Asatru Community Association website, 2008, http://www.socalasatru.org/Dec08_00.html

14 Orderic of Vitalis quoted in Joynes, A., *Medieval Ghost Stories: An Anthology of Miracles, Marvels And Prodigies*, Boydell Press, 2001, p.68.

15 Plischke (1914) and Röhrich (1967) in Davidson, H.E., 'The Wild Hunt: Stories from the South West of Ireland' in Davidson, H. and Chaudhri, A., *Supernatural Enemies*, Carolina Academic Press, 2001.

16 De Vries (1932) in Davidson, H.E. (ibid.).

17 Thanks to Juha Niesniemi who has summarised a variety of Finnish sources to give me this research and much of the material on the Staalo in a few pages time.

18 '*Rare Exports*: Interview with Finnish director Jalmari Helander', Bloodydisgusting.com, http://www.bloody-disgusting.com/news/22604 retrieved 23/01/12.

CHAPTER FIVE

19 Andersen, A., 'Icelandic Christmas through the ages', Reykjavic Grapevine, 03/01/11, http://www.grapevine.is/Features/Read Article/Slice-of-Icelandic-Christmas-Through-the-Ages

20 I have written this version of the 'Christmas Cat' by taking an online translation of the text by Vignir Jonnson (http://www.simnet.is/gardarj/yule11.htm) and attempting to re-write it so that it scans as a poem and captures the intent, tone and feel of Jóhannes úr Kötlum's poem. I'd like to thank Gudjon Olaffson and William Vaughan for their invaluable advice and guidance in doing this, as I don't speak a word of Icelandic! Unfortunately, due to this linguistic barrier, I have been unable to ascertain who the rights-holders are to Jóhannes_úr_Kötlum's estate in order to discuss my intentions with them, for which I sincerely apologise. I believe that what I have created is a re-interpretation rather than a direct translation, but I very much hope that I have done justice to the original and that no copyright has been infringed by attempts to capture the spirit of his work. However, I felt it would be a disservice to the role and importance of úr Kötlum's poem in Icelandic Christmas folklore if I did not discuss the poem and attempt to demonstrate its tone and impact.

CHAPTER SEVEN

21 Plutarch, *Life of Caesar*, Loeb Classical Library Edition, 1919, p.585.

22 Lucian, *Lucian IV*, trans. K. Kilburn, quoted in Forbes, B.D., *Christmas: A Candid History*, University of California Press, 2007, p.6.

23 'Asterius of Amasea, Sermons (1904), Preface to the online edition', Roger Pearse (translator), Ipswich, UK, December 2003, webpage: ECWritings-Aste. Retrieved from http://www.tertullian.org/fathers/asterius_04_sermon4.htm

24 Faculty of Theology in Paris, 1444, quoted in Harris, M., *Sacred Folly: A New History of the Feast of Fools*, Cornell University Press, 2011, pp.1–2.

25 Lebeuf, *Memoires*, quoted in Harris (ibid.).

26 'Treatise Against Dicing', reprinted in Brand, J. and Ellis, H., *The Popular Antiquities of Great Britain* Largely Extended, Corrected, Brought Down To The Present Time, and Now First Alphabetically Arranged. Reeves and Turner, 1905, pp.427–9

27 It is worth bearing in mind that Hugo was writing about events 200 years earlier so may be an unreliable narrator.

CHAPTER EIGHT

28 Woodhead, I., 'Babushka and the Three Kings: A Christmas Tale but not Russian', Suite 101, 25/03/13, http://suite101.com/article/babushka-and-the-three-kings—-a-christmas-tale-but-not-russian-a313464

CHAPTER NINE

29 Golby and Purdue in Forbes, B.D., *Christmas: A Candid History*, University of California Press, 2007, p.58.

30 Paxman, J., Empire: What Ruling the World Did to the British, Viking, 2012, pp. 120–1.

31 'Christmas story-teller', London, 1878, p.215, quoted in Connelly, M., *Christmas: A Social History*, I.B. Tauris, 1999, p.13.

32 *New York Herald*, 1839, quoted in Bowles, G., *The World Encyclopaedia of Christmas*, McClelland and Stewart, 2000, p.233.

33 There is a school of thought that links between Santa Claus and reindeer come from the rituals of Sami shamans in Lapland, the Arctic and Siberia. However, as these rituals were not well known in America at the time there is no convincing evidence of a link between the two.

CHAPTER TEN

34 Nast, T. and Nast St Hill, T., *Thomas Nast's Christmas Drawings*, Dover Publications, 1978.

35 Jon Ronson, 'Santa's Little Conspirators' in *Lost at Sea: The Jon Ronson Mysteries*, Croydon, Picador, 2012.

36 Irvine, I., 'Btw', the *Independent,* 26/11/05, http://www.independent.co.uk/voices/commentators/ian-irvine-btw-516988.html

37 http://www.spellingmistakescostlives.com/santa/index.htm retrieved 27/01/12.

38 The *Sun* newspaper, 29/04/05.

39 Macrae, F., 'Is this crude ad really the best way to tackle unwanted pregnancies?' the *Daily Mail*, 28/11/08, http://www.dailymail.co.uk/femail/article-1090080/Is-crude-ad-really-best-way-tackle-unwanted-pregnancies-Christmas.html#ixzz2TRGQZ85V

40 http://www.politifreak.com/naughty-or-nice-nyc-santa-claus-passes-out-needles-condoms/

41 http://newsjustforyou1.blogspot.co.uk/2012/12/a-new-low-for-ny-ny-health-clinic-video.html

402 http://newsbusters.org/blogs/paul-wilson/2012/12/18/samsung-ad-shows-sexting-santa

43 http://www.idownloadblog.com/2012/12/17/samsung-christmas-2012-ad/

44 http://blogs.detroitnews.com/poptropolis/2012/12/18/samsungs-naughty-mrs-claus-ad-is-the-worst-commercial-of-the-year/

CONCLUSION

45 Belk, Russell W. (1987), 'A Child's Christmas in America: Santa Claus as Deity, Consumption as 'Religion', *Journal of American Culture*, 10/1987/100.

46 Carter, S., Christmas Past, Christmas Present: 400 Years of English Seasonal Customs 1600–2000, Geffrye Museum, 1997, p.5.

Index

Valkyries, 89
Van Es, Andrée, 50
Victoria, Queen, 184
Victorians, Christmas revived
    by, 7, 184
Virgin Mary, 192
'Visit from St Nicholas, A' (a.k.a.
    'The Night Before
    Christmas') (Moore), 20,
    119, 202
  disputed authorship of, 203
Visit from Santa Claus, The, 214

Walchelin, 86–7
Waldensians, 159
wassailing, 149–51, 188
'We Wish You a Merry
    Christmas', 150
Weinnachtsmann, see Christmas
    Man
Wild Hunt, 82–91, 142, 155, 159
  origins of, 88–91
  shifting traditions of, 162
Wilde, Oscar, 128
William the Evil, 42
Window Peeper, 112
  see also Yule Lads
Wise Men, see Three Kings

witch trials, 69, 161–2
Woden, see Odin
Woodhead, Irene, 177
Woods, Samuel, 201
World War One, 174
Wrenboys, 154–5
Wrong Santa Claus, The, 215
Wycliffe, John, 163

Yule, 7, 12, 228
  Christians co-opt, 13, 84
  and Tulya's Eve, 92
  see also Christmas
Yule Goat, 94–9
  roots of, 96
Yule Lads, 9, 14, 109–14, 178,
    208, 216, 235
  banning of, 162
  and Christmas Cat, 115
  cruelty of, 110
  new image sought for, 123
  new outfits for, 219
  public decree concerning,
    113–14
  in twentieth century, 118–19,
    122–3

Zwarte Piet, see Black Peter